THE HIGH-ENERGY COOKBOOK

4522

This edition published 1997 by Strathearn Books Limited

© 1997 CLB International,

a division of Quadrillion Publishing Ltd,

Godalming Business Centre, Woolsack Way, Godalming,

Surrey, England GU7 1XW

Printed and bound in Italy by New Interlitho Italia S.P.A.

ISBN 1-85833-562-0

NUTRITIONAL CONSULTANCY by Jill Scott

PROJECT MANAGEMENT by Jo Richardson

PRODUCED by Anthology

ORIGINAL DESIGN CONCEPT by Roger Hyde

DESIGN MANAGEMENT by Rhoda Nottridge

PAGE MAKE-UP by Vanessa Good

PHOTOGRAPHY by Don Last;

Sheila Terry – *jacket, pages 14-5 (top), 22-3, 39, 48, 62-3*

(home economy by Anne Sheasby)

HOME ECONOMY by Joy Parker; Christine France

PRODUCTION by Ruth Arthur, Karen Staff,

Neil Randles and Paul Randles

THE HIGH-ENERGY COOKBOOK

TASTY & HEALTHY RECIPES FOR ENHANCING EVERYDAY ENERGY AND VITALITY

Anne Sheasby

STRATHEARN BOOKS LIMITED
Toronto, Canada

CONTENTS

INTRODUCTION

*C*hoosing *the right balance of foods helps to make us feel more energetic, stay healthy, and creates a sense of well-being. If you enjoy your food, have a busy lifestyle, and want to get the most out of life, then this book is for you.*

The High Energy cookbook offers delicious, mouthwatering recipes to suit all tastes, based on sound nutritional principles; easy-to-read information about the relationship between food, nutrition, and health, based on the latest international scientific reports; practical advice on nutrition, for example, how to create a good eating plan for life.

The High Energy Cookbook is aimed at anyone who is trying to make healthy lifestyle changes, particularly in relation to diet and exercise, as well as those people looking to maximize their energy levels, not only to cope with the stresses and strains of everyday life, but also to enjoy life to the full. People who have physically demanding occupations or who have to work long hours will also benefit from the healthy, energy-giving options presented in this book, together with those engaged in sports, fitness, and leisure activities or thinking about taking up some form of physical activity.

The book is aimed at adults and older children, but the principles and recipes are suitable for children over the age of five.

THE BALANCE OF GOOD HEALTH

Diet has long been recognized as an important contributor to health and to the prevention of life-threatening diseases, particularly coronary heart disease and stroke. Eating the right types, combinations, and amounts of foods is important for health for a variety of reasons, including
- less risk of becoming overweight
- less risk of developing heart disease and some cancers
- fewer bowel disorders

One practical way to ensure you are obtaining all the nutrients your body needs is to choose a variety of foods from the major food groups every day. No single food contains all nutrients; different foods are rich in different nutrients. It is the total diet that is either healthy or unhealthy rather than specific foods, although some foods contribute more to healthy eating than others.

Within each food group, it is not only the quantity of foods eaten but also the type of foods chosen that is important for good health. The table opposite indicates the nutrients provided by the different food groups, the healthier options, and an indication of how much you need from each group.

The recipes in this book are specifically designed to fit within these guidelines, so that the choices you make are healthy ones.

FOOD GROUPS

FOOD GROUP AND ITS MAIN NUTRIENTS	TYPES OF FOODS TO CHOOSE MOST OFTEN	HOW MUCH TO CHOOSE
FRUITS AND VEGETABLES *Provide: vitamins, e.g. vitamin C; carotenes; folates; some minerals; and dietary fiber.*	*All types. Eat a wide variety of fresh, frozen, and canned; dried fruits and fruit juices.*	*Aim for at least five servings daily, e.g. orange juice at breakfast; salad in a sandwich at lunch; banana to follow; 2 servings of vegetables with evening meal.*
BREAD, PASTA, RICE, OTHER GRAINS, AND POTATOES *Provide: energy; some protein, calcium, and iron; B vitamins. Whole-grain varieties are higher in fiber.*	*Whole-grain varieties of bread, pasta, rice, pita bread, breakfast cereals; Boiled, baked, or mashed potato.*	*Should be the entrée in every meal. Eat lots!*
MILK AND DAIRY FOODS *Includes milk, yogurt, yellow cheese, and cottage cheese. Provide: calcium, protein, vitamins A & D; vitamin B 12.*	*Lower fat varieties, e.g. skim, 2%, or low-fat milk; low-fat yogurts or low-fat cheeses.*	*Eat or dink moderate amounts: as a guide — 2-3 servings daily (e.g. 1 carton yogurt, 1 cup milk, 1 ounce cheese).*
MEAT, FISH, AND ALTERNATIVES *Includes meat, poultry, fish, eggs, nuts, beans, and legumes. Provide: iron, protein, B vitamins; minerals including zinc and magnesium.*	*Lean cuts of meat; all types of fish (not coated); beans, peas, and lentils are low in fat, high in fiber: use in stews, chili, and casseroles.*	*Eat moderate amounts: as a guide — 2-3 servings daily (e.g. 2-3 ounces meat, 4-5 ounces fish, 1 cup beans/legumes; 2 ounces cheese).*
FOODS CONTAINING FAT; FOODS CONTAINING SUGAR *Includes: fat spreads, i.e. butter, margarine, low-fat spreads; oils; dressings; cream; mayonnaise; cookies; savory snacks; sweets and sugar. Provides: energy and some vitamins and essential fatty acids. Also contain a lot of fat, sugar, and salt.*	*Low-fat spreads, or small amounts of other sour spreads. Use unsaturated oil in cooking, e.g. pure vegetable oils, olive, sunflower, safflower, etc.*	*Small amounts of spreading/cooking fats daily. Savory snacks, cakes, cream, etc. only occasionally.*

FOODS FOR GOOD HEALTH

A number of foods, including fruits and vegetables, are particularly important for good health, since they are known to protect people from chronic illness such as coronary disease and some cancers. Here we explain why these "superfoods" are so good for you. Turn to page 70 and the beginning of Chapter Seven for some delicious recipes using a variety of fruits and vegetables.

ANTIOXIDANTS AND HEALTH

The antioxidant vitamins are beta-carotene, sometimes known as provitamin A because it can be converted to vitamin A in the body, vitamins C, and E (often referred to as the "ACE" vitamins). Certain minerals have antioxidant properties — selenium, zinc, manganese, and copper. They work together to destroy the so-called "free radicals," and thus protect body cells from damage. Compounds called flavenoids, which can be found in red wine, tea, and onions, may also have antioxidant properties.

Free radicals are produced in the body as the by-product of normal metabolism. They can also be taken into the body, for instance through cigarette smoke, and other environmental pollutants such as exhaust fumes or radiation.

Free radicals are highly reactive, unstable compounds which can cause damage to the genetic make-up (DNA) of cells if left unchecked. In order to protect cells against free radical attacks, the body has developed a series of protective mechanisms which involve the "ACE" vitamins.

BETA-CAROTENE OR PROVITAMIN A can be converted to vitamin A in the body. However, beta-carotene is also a powerful antioxidant in its own right. It is fat soluble and appears to help protect fatty parts of cells.
VITAMIN C is a water-soluble vitamin. It "mops up" free radicals, and is also able to help regenerate vitamin E.
VITAMIN E is thought to be the first line of defense against damage to the fatty parts of the cell. Populations with low blood levels of vitamin E have been shown to have a higher risk of heart disease.

The antioxidant minerals described above (selenium, zinc, etc.) are found in a wide range of foods, particularly whole-grain cereals, nuts, meat, milk, and other dairy products.

FOOD SOURCES OF ANTIOXIDANT VITAMINS

BETA-CAROTENE/PROVITAMIN A Bright yellow and orange fruits and green vegetables; carrots; apricots; peaches; tomatoes; red and yellow bell peppers; green leaf vegetables.
VITAMIN C Citrus fruits and juices; kiwi fruits; blueberries; acerola; strawberries; green bell peppers; tomatoes; green leaf vegetables; new potatoes.
VITAMIN E Vegetable oils (particularly sunflower); almonds; hazelnuts; whole-grain breakfast cereals and bread; green leaf vegetables; avocados; eggs; cheese and other dairy products; margarine.

FIVE-A-DAY FOR HEALTH

Eating a healthy, well-balanced diet that is low in fat, with plenty of fruits and vegetables, is one of the best ways to help protect you and your family from coronary heart disease and cancer. The research evidence that fruits and vegetables have an important protective effect on a wide range of cancers is strong, consistent, and universally accepted.

Leading health organizations recommend consuming at least five servings of different fruits and vegetables every day. For many people, this represents about a 50% increase from current intakes.
ONE SERVING OF FRUIT IS EQUIVALENT TO: one piece of fruit, e.g. a large slice of melon, or an apple; a wineglass of fruit juice (about $1/2$ cup); 1 tbsp of dried fruits, or $1/2$ cup stewed or canned fruits.
ONE SERVING OF VEGETABLES IS EQUIVALENT TO: two heaped tbsp (approximately 3 ounces) of green or root vegetables, three serving spoons of peas or corn, or a bowl of green salad.

Nature packages a range of different nutrients into fruits and vegetables, so it is important to eat a variety every day in order to maximize your intake of vitamins, minerals, and fiber.

TIPS FOR RETAINING VITAMINS AND MINERALS

- Wash/scrub vegetables rather than peel, where possible.
- Prepare vegetables just before cooking; do not soak them in water prior to cooking.
- Add prepared vegetables to the minimum of boiling water and cook briefly, so that they sill have "crunch."
- Never add baking soda to cooking water.
- Eat raw, steamed, microwaved, or stir-fried vegetables whenever possible, to minimize vitamin losses.
- Serve cooked vegetables immediately — keeping them warm rapidly destroys the vitamin C.
- Frozen fruits and vegetables are as nutritious as fresh, and many even contain more vitamin C.

THE IMPORTANCE OF DIETARY FIBER

There are two types of dietary fiber: insoluble and soluble.

Insoluble fiber is generally found in whole-grain cereals, such as wheat and rye, and is not absorbed or digested by the human body. This form of fiber is important for healthy bowels, and can help protect you from constipation and other bowel problems.

Soluble fiber is found mainly in fruits and vegetables, as well as in oatmeal, and some forms of this fiber can be absorbed into the digestive system. Recent evidence suggests that soluble fiber can help lower blood cholesterol levels, and therefore is useful in protecting the body against heart disease.

We need to consume around 12-18g (about half an ounce) of fiber a day for good health. This dietary fiber should consist of a mixture of cereal fiber, oat bran fiber, beans, and legumes, as well as a variety of fruits and vegetables. Check the nutrition panels on each recipe in the book to monitor your daily fiber intake.

FATS AND HEALTH

A small amount of fat in the diet is important for good health and makes food tastier. Consuming too much fat, however, is associated with obesity, heart disease, and the development of some cancers. Throughout The High-Energy Cookbook, the levels of fat in each recipe are within the international recommended guidelines of no more than 30-35% dietary energy from fat.

Achieving a healthy balance of both the total amount of fat intake in your diet, as well as the type of fat, is an important part of healthy eating. There are three main types of fat: saturated, monounsaturated, and polyunsaturated fats.

SATURATED FATS: These are not essential in the diet, and a high intake is associated with a higher risk of developing heart disease. Saturated fats can raise blood cholesterol levels, so it is a good idea to keep your intake of these fats low.

DIETARY SOURCES OF SATURATED FATS:
● full-fat dairy products (whole milk, cream, sour cream, hard, and soft cheese)
● fatty cuts of red meat and red meat products, such as ground meats and hamburgers, sausages, and sausage patties
● butter and other spreading fats
● foods containing "hidden" fats, including cakes, cookies, snacks, ice cream, and candy

MONOUNSATURATED FATS: Recent studies have shown that monounsaturated fats are effective at lowering blood cholesterol, so they can help protect against the development of heart disease. In the countries of the Mediterranean, such as southern Italy and Greece, where the diet is fairly high in fat (mainly from olive oil, which is rich in monounsaturates) but low in saturated fat, the inhabitants have a very low incidence of heart disease. It is thought that a diet rich in mono-unsaturates, combined with a high intake of fruits and vegetables, may protect these populations from heart disease.

DIETARY SOURCES OF MONOUNSATURATED FATS:
● Olive oil, peanut oil, canola oil, and fat spreads made from these oils
● nuts (brazils, pecans, and pistachios)
● seeds (sesame)
● meat (lamb, beef, and chicken)

POLYUNSATURATED FATS: Small amounts of these fats are essential for good health. Some can also be helpful at lowering blood cholesterol levels.

Dietary sources of polyunsaturated fats:
● vegetable oils, especially safflower, sunflower, soya, and corn oil
● margarines and spreads labeled "high in polyunsaturates"
● some nuts (pine nuts, walnuts, and brazil nuts) and seeds (sesame)

THE HEALTHY FAT PLAN
● Choose a low-fat spread or a spread high in unsaturated fats, instead of butter.
● Use skim, low-fat, or 2% milk instead of full cream milk.
● Buy the leanest cuts of red meat you can afford; cut away any visible fat.
● Eat fish more often, including oil-rich fish. Broil, microwave, steam, or bake it rather than sautéing or frying it.
● When you use oil for cooking, use it sparingly, and choose one high in unsaturates, such as olive oil, canola, sunflower, or corn oil.
● Choose healthy snacks, such as fresh fruits, corn tortillas, or English muffins, instead of cakes, cookies, and pastries.

FOODS FOR ENERGY

Whether you are physically active through work or exercise, or just lead a busy life, you will need energy. Energy is supplied in different amounts by the food we eat.

Carbohydrates and fats supply most of the energy needed for exercise and physical activity. Although fat provides more than twice the amount of energy per unit weight than carbohydrate, it is carbohydrate that is the most important fuel for exercise, because this is the most accessible form of energy for your working muscles. The recipes in this book are all high in carbohydrate to keep your energy levels high, whether for exercise or sport, or if you lead a busy lifestyle or have a demanding job.

It may be helpful to eat small, frequent meals rather than three main meals, especially if you are on the move all the time. If you exercise regularly, make sure that you eat (or drink) a carbohydrate-rich snack or meal within one to two hours after exercising, to maximize your refueling.

Here we present two illustrated examples of everyday meals, showing quick and easy ways of boosting their carbohydrate content.

1 fresh banana, peeled and sliced

HIGH-ENERGY BRAN FLAKES
4 tbsp bran flakes, skim milk, low-fat, or 2% milk, or low-fat plain yogurt, plus any one or more of the following:

4 tbsp ready-to-eat dried apricots

2 tbsp dried apple rings, chopped

4 tbsp raisins/4 tbsp yellow raisins

HIGH-ENERGY SNACKS

- Banana Sandwich (2 slices bread)
- 3 small Bananas
- Homemade Bran Muffin, such as Pineapple Bran Muffins (*page 29*)
- Fruit Bars (*page 29*)
- 1/3 cup Dried Fruits, such as raisins
- 6 Crispbreads with 1 tbsp Honey

- 1 x 8-ounce baked jacket potato with low-fat topping (*page 56*)
- Bowl of Cereal (such as 1/2 cup granola or whole-wheat, sugarless cereal) with skim milk
- Salad Sandwich and one piece of Fruit

- Bowl of Fruit Salad with a small carton of Low-Fat, Fruit-flavored Yogurt
- Bowl of Potato & Carrot Soup with Whole-wheat Bread Roll (*page 52*)
- Raisin & Lemon Cookies (*page 28*)
- Fruit & Spice Coffeecake (*page 23*)

CARBOHYDRATE BOOSTERS

● Plan all your meals and snacks around a carbohydrate-rich food, so that more than half your plate is filled with it. It could be a low-fat sauce on a bed of pasta; a baked potato with low-fat filling; thick sandwiches, or a pita pocket with a small amount of filling. Serve extra bread with other dishes, such as pizzas and pasta dishes.

● Experiment with different pastas and noodles, adding a variety of sauces, especially vegetable-based ones which are low in fat. Try adding kidney beans or lentils in place of meat, such as Lamb & Lentil Casserole (page 67) or the Chicken Medley (page 68).

● Enjoy plenty of fresh fruits, or try canned fruits in natural juice for a change. Add dried fruits to breakfast cereals to boost carbohydrates and fiber.

● Breakfast cereals can be a nutritious snack at any time of the day. Choose high-fiber, low-sugar varieties whenever possible, and serve with skim milk or 2% milk.

● Cakes, cookies, and candies are high in fat. Choose bread-based snacks, speciality breads, and rolls (but not croissants), and spread them with jelly, jam, honey, or preserves and a scraping of low-fat spread.

HIGH-ENERGY SMOKED CHICKEN &
MUSHROOM RISOTTO
(recipe on page 48)
This risotto using cooked, skinless and boneless smoked chicken, mushrooms, and peas, has been boosted to "high-energy" status by:
– *increasing the quantity of rice and slightly reducing the quantity of chicken*
– *adding some frozen fava beans along with the peas*
– *adding some canned, drained chick-peas (garbanzo beans)*
– *adding some yellow raisins*

Choose from a wide variety of delicious breads to serve with your meal, for an extra energy booster.

HIGH-ENERGY SIDE DISHES

a baked potato with delicious crispy skin, garnished with sprigs of fresh herbs and served with mixed salad leaves

a mixture of standard and sweet potatoes, sliced, tossed in a little olive oil, and open-roasted on a cookie sheet

boiled baby new potatoes tossed in chopped mixed fresh herbs

cooked couscous mixed with chopped fresh herbs and chopped green onions (scallions)

cooked long-grain and wild rice, mixed together and garnished with fresh herbs

cooked brown long-grain rice mixed with diced red, yellow, and green bell peppers, chopped red onion, and cooked corn kernels

15

With so much information, and so many recipes to choose from, how do you pull all this together to suit your individual needs? We all have different energy (calorie) requirements, and it is that which should determine the total amount of food we eat. Factors that affect individual energy needs include:

● gender — women tend to need less energy than men
● age — older adults need less energy than teenagers and young adults
● weight — less energy is required to achieve a healthy weight
● physical activity — the more active you are, the greater your energy needs

In addition, we all have our own likes and dislikes and our own lifestyles, which can affect when and what we eat. However, there may be some important points to consider for different lifestyles, and some suggested options are given here, using the recipes in the book.

PEOPLE WITH PHYSICALLY DEMANDING JOBS

If you are constantly on the move at work, you need plenty of energy to keep you going. You may be using up a lot of energy during the day, and you need to replace this mainly through starchy, carbohydrate-rich foods. Eating regularly is important for everyone, and you may also need snacks in between.

Breakfast
Whole-grain breakfast cereal with sliced banana and skim milk; orange juice; whole-wheat toast with low-fat spread and jam or honey.

Mid-morning
Drink (tea, coffee, or diet drink); Raisin & Lemon Cookies (page 28).

Lunch
Corn, Leek, & Mushroom Pizza (pages 30-31) served with thick, crusty bread and a side salad; low-fat fruit-flavored yogurt; fresh fruit.

Mid-afternoon
Drink (as above); Pineapple Bran Muffins (page 29).

Evening meal
Tuna & Shrimp Risotto (page 49) served with Cheese, Herb, & Onion Bread (page 19) and a mixed salad; Banana Apricot Fool (page 75).

PEOPLE WITH BUSY OFFICE JOBS

Eating regularly is still important, particularly starting the day with a breakfast. If you need snacks between meals, opt for fresh fruit or a healthy, high-carbohydrate snack.

Breakfast
Whole-grain cereal with skim or low-fat milk; fruit juice; toast or bread with jam or jelly.

Mid-morning
Fresh fruit; drink (as before).

Lunch
Club Sandwich (page 21); low-fat plain yogurt; fresh fruit.

Mid-afternoon
Drink; fresh fruit or a slice of Banana & Ginger Loaf (page 24).

Evening meal
Chili & Macaroni Bake (page 40) served with green vegetables and Sun-dried Tomato & Olive Soda Bread (page 20); Spicy Fruit Compote (page 74).

PHYSICALLY ACTIVE PEOPLE (including sportspeople)

It is likely that you will already be eating regularly, to satisfy your hearty appetite! Make sure you fill up on low-fat, high-carbohydrate snacks to help keep muscle glycogen stores topped up. Remember to drink plenty of the right kind of fluids throughout the day (see opposite).

Breakfast
Fruit Compote (e.g. Peach & Pear, page 75); large bowl of whole-grain cereal with low-fat milk; fruit juice; toast or bread; Whole-wheat Raisin & Orange Muffins (page 22) and jam or jelly.

Mid-morning
Cheese & Pear Scones (page 27) with low-fat spread and jam or honey; drink (as before).

Lunch
Large baked potato with Spicy Tomato & Mushroom topping (page 56) served with a mixed salad such as Red Bean & Three-Mushroom Salad (page 63); Fruit & Spice Coffeecake (page 23) or Fruit Bars (page 29); fresh fruits.

Mid-afternoon
Banana Berry Shake (page 76).

Evening meal
Beef & Bean Burgers (page 65) served in a whole-wheat roll with mixed vegetables; Steamed Chocolate & Cherry Pudding (page 72).

Supper
Drink (as before); Carrot & Raisin Cake (page 73).

DRINKS AND FLUIDS

Drinking enough of the right types of fluid is just as important as eating the right amount and types of food for good health. Maintaining fluid balance is particularly important when you are physically active.

Whenever you exercise, you lose some fluid, mainly through sweating. How much you lose depends on how hard you exercise or train, how long you exercise and train for, and the air temperature and relative humidity. If you tend to sweat easily, you need to take extra care to ensure you are fully hydrated before exercise, especially in hot weather.

Losing fluid through sweating is an effective way to regulate body temperature. However, even small losses of body water can impair your sports performance, especially in prolonged exercise, so it is essential to be well hydrated before you start. Filling up with fluids during exercise helps to prevent dehydration. Try practicing this during exercise or training sessions, taking small amounts of fluid at regular intervals. Aim eventually to drink approximately ¹/₂ to ²/₃ cup of fluid every 15 minutes.

It is difficult to drink too much, but easy to drink too little! Aim for a minimum of 8 cups (1 quart) fluid a day — more to replace fluid losses during exercise. Suitable fluids include water, fruit juices, sugarless concentrates to be mixed with water, tea, and coffee (in small amounts, or try the decaffeinated versions). Fluids can also be used to replace carbohydrate losses during exercise. Turn to page 76 for recipes for two nutritious and refreshing drinks.

NUTRITIONAL ANALYSES

Nutritional information for each recipe in the book is provided in easy-reference panels. The nutritional figures are per serving of the recipe in each case, and do not include any serving suggestions that may be included in the introduction or at the end of a recipe, unless specifically stated otherwise in the nutritional panel. These analyses have been compiled as accurately as possible, but the nutritional content of the foods will vary depending on their source.

As well as specifying the number of calories per serving, the nutritional analysis also gives the overall fat content, which is then broken down into the three fat types: saturates, monounsaturates, and polyunsaturates. Your intake of fat, especially saturates, should be kept low for good health.

The analysis also gives the percentage of calories from fat, which should be no more than 30-35% for good health, as well as the percentage of energy from saturated fat. In a healthy diet, the latter should not exceed 10%.

Recommendations are that for good health over 50-55% of dietary energy, or calories in the diet, should be provided by carbohydrates, and the percentage of total calories from carbohydrates is given for each recipe in the analyses.

Figures for the sodium content of each recipe are also included. This figure does not include any salt that is added to the recipe during preparation and cooking.

Where a nutritional analysis states that a recipe is a good source of a particular vitamin, mineral, or other nutrient, this indicates that a serving of the recipe will make a significant contribution to the recommended daily allowance (RDA) of the nutrients.

A GUIDE TO THE RECIPES

● All spoon measurements refer to American Standard measuring spoons, and all measurements given are for level spoons.

● The cooking times for all the recipes in this book are based on the oven or broiler being preheated.

● All eggs used in the recipes are medium (weighing 21 ounces per dozen) eggs.

KEY TO SYMBOLS

 Suitable for freezing.

 Suitable for cooking in a microwave oven.

 Suitable for vegetarians.

Please note that the term vegetarian applies to lacto-ovo vegetarians, i.e. people who eat eggs and dairy products but not meat, fish, and poultry, nor any products derived from these foods.

CHAPTER ONE

BREADS

*B*read has been part of the staple diet of many countries for thousands of years, and is a most nutritious and versatile food that can be eaten and enjoyed at any time of the day. It is healthy, wholesome, and filling, and is available in many delicious varieties. As a good source of carbohydrate, bread is also low in fat and contains some B vitamins, calcium, and iron. The whole-wheat varieties are also high in fiber.

When making or choosing sandwiches, watch out for high-fat fillings and choose reduced-fat alternatives for foods such as cheese, mayonnaise, and coleslaw. Use fat spread sparingly and choose low- or reduced-fat spreads in preference to butter or margarine. Fill sandwiches with plenty of fresh vegetables or salad ingredients for extra flavor and nutrients.

BRAIDED CHEESE & POPPYSEED BREAD

Try serving this bread with a bowl of hot homemade soup.

Preparation time: 20 minutes, plus kneading and rising time

Cooking time: 35-45 minutes

Makes one 1¹/₂-pound loaf (10 slices)

4 cups all-purpose flour
2 tbsp soft margarine
¹/₃ cup finely shredded sharp Cheddar cheese
2 tsp mustard powder
1¹/₂ tsp salt
freshly ground black pepper
1 tbsp fresh yeast or 1 envelope active dry yeast
1¹/₄ cups lukewarm low-fat or 2% milk,
for glazing
poppyseeds, for sprinkling

1 Place the flour in a large bowl and rub in the margarine. Add the cheese, mustard, salt, and pepper, mix well and make a well in the center.

2 Blend the yeast and milk together. Add the yeast liquid to the dry ingredients and mix well to form a soft but not sticky dough.

3 Turn onto a floured surface and knead for about 10 minutes, until the dough feels smooth and elastic. Shape into a round, place in a bowl, and cover with a clean kitchen towel. Leave to rise in a warm place for about 45 minutes, until doubled in size.

4 Turn onto a floured surface and knead again for about 5 minutes, until smooth and elastic. Divide, and roll the dough into two strands. Place side by side and pinch together at one end. Loosely braid the strands, then pinch them together at the other end. Place on a lightly floured baking sheet.

5 Cover with a clean kitchen towel and leave to rise in a warm place for about 30 minutes. Brush with milk to glaze and sprinkle with some poppyseeds.

6 Bake in a preheated oven at 375° for 35-45 minutes, until well-risen and golden brown. Cover the bread with foil if it is browning too much. Transfer to a wire rack to cool.

NUTRITIONAL ANALYSIS

(figures are per slice)

Calories = 225
Fat = 6.7g
of which saturates = 2.7g
      monounsaturates = 1.7g
      polyunsaturates = 1.8g
Protein = 9.0g
Carbohydrate = 35.6g
Dietary fiber = 1.4g
Sodium = 0.4g

Percentage of total calories from fat = 27%
of which saturates = 10%
Percentage of total calories from carbohydrate = 59%, of which sugars = 4%

CHEESE, HERB, & ONION
BREAD

This bread is quick and easy to make, with delicious results.
Serve it warm or cold as a snack, for a sandwich, or to accompany
a meal such as a pasta dish or salad.

Preparation time: 25 minutes
Cooking time: 1-1¼ hours
Makes one 2-pound loaf (12 slices)

1 large onion, minced
2 cups all-purpose flour
2 cups whole-wheat flour
1 tsp double-acting baking powder
2 tsp salt
freshly ground black pepper
2 tsp mustard powder
¼ cup soft margarine
⅔ cup finely shredded reduced-fat sharp Cheddar cheese
4 tbsp minced fresh mixed herbs or 1 tbsp dried mixed herbs
2 eggs, beaten
1¼ cups low-fat or 2% milk

1 Dry-fry the onion in a heavy-based nonstick skillet for 5 minutes.

2 Mix the flours, baking powder, salt, pepper, and mustard powder in a bowl. Rub in the margarine until the mixture resembles fine bread crumbs.

Add the cheese, herbs, and onion and mix well.

3 Add the eggs and milk and mix together thoroughly. Turn the dough mixture into a lightly greased 2-pound loaf pan and level the surface.

4 Bake in a preheated oven at 375° for 1-1¼ hours, until risen and golden brown.

5 Turn out and cool on a wire rack. Serve warm or cold in slices.

VARIATIONS

● Halve the quantities if you would like to make a 1-pound loaf, or divide the mixture between two 1-pound loaf pans and bake for slightly less time.
● Use other reduced-fat hard cheeses, such as Monterey jack or Swiss, in place of the Cheddar cheese.
● Use all white all-purpose or whole-wheat flour in place of the mixture.

NUTRITIONAL ANALYSIS

(figures are per slice)

Calories = 219
Fat = 7.5g
of which saturates = 2.3g
      monounsaturates = 2.1g
      polyunsaturates = 2.4g

Protein = 10.4g
Carbohydrate = 29.2g
Dietary fiber = 2.6g
Sodium = 0.5g

Percentage of total calories from fat = 31%
of which saturates = 9%
Percentage of total calories from carbohydrate = 50%, of which sugars = 5%

SUN-DRIED TOMATO & OLIVE
SODA BREAD

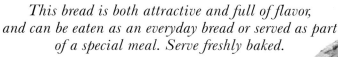

This bread is both attractive and full of flavor, and can be eaten as an everyday bread or served as part of a special meal. Serve freshly baked.

Preparation time: 20 minutes
Cooking time: 30-40 minutes
Serves 8 (8 wedges)

4 cups all-purpose flour
3 tsp double-acting baking soda
1 tsp salt
freshly ground black pepper
2 tsp dried mixed herbs
¹/₄ cup soft margarine
¹/₃ cup sun-dried tomatoes in olive oil, drained thoroughly and finely chopped
¹/₃ cup pitted black olives, drained thoroughly and finely chopped
1¹/₄ cups buttermilk

1 Sift the flour and double-acting baking powder into a bowl, add the salt, pepper, and herbs and mix well. Rub in the margarine until the mixture resembles fine bread crumbs.

2 Add the chopped tomatoes and olives and mix well. Add the buttermilk and mix to a soft dough. Knead lightly, shape into an 8-inch round, and place on a lightly greased baking sheet. Mark the round into 8 even wedges.

3 Bake in a preheated oven at 400° for 30-40 minutes, until risen and golden brown. Serve warm or cold, cut into wedges.

VARIATIONS
● Replace all or half of the all-purpose flour with whole-wheat flour.
● Use whole, low-fat, or 2% milk in place of the buttermilk.

NUTRITIONAL ANALYSIS
(figures are per wedge)

Calories = 300
Fat = 11.1g
of which saturates = 1.9g
      monounsaturates = 3.2g
      polyunsaturates = 5.0g

Protein = 6.8g
Carbohydrate = 45.9g
Dietary fiber = 2.1g
Sodium = 0.7g

Percentage of total calories from fat = 33%, of which saturates = 6%
Percentage of total calories from carbohydrate = 57%, of which sugars = 4%

CLUB SANDWICH

Preparation time: 15 minutes

Cooking time: 5 minutes

Serves 2

2 slices lean smoked bacon, trimmed
5 tsp reduced-calorie mayonnaise
5 tsp low-fat plain yogurt
6 thick slices whole-wheat bread
2 slices (2 ounces) cooked, skinless,
boneless chicken breast
$^1/_3$ cup drained canned corn kernels
2 tbsp yellow raisins
shredded crisp lettuce
salt and freshly ground black pepper
1 tomato, sliced
2 tbsp chopped watercress

1 Broil the bacon until crispy, then chop or slice it.

2 Meanwhile, combine the mayonnaise and yogurt. Place two slices of bread on individual plates and spread each with some of the mayonnaise mixture.

3 Place the chicken, corn, yellow raisins, and lettuce over the mayonnaise, season, and top each with another slice of bread.

4 Spread these slices of bread with the mayonnaise mixture and place the bacon, tomato, and watercress on top.

5 Top each with a third slice of bread to make two club sandwiches.

6 Press lightly together and cut in half diagonally, then in half again to make quarters. Serve immediately.

VARIATIONS
● Use other breads such as white, mixed-grain, or rye bread.
● Sprinkle some minced fresh herbs over the fillings.
● Use unsmoked bacon in place of the smoked bacon.

NUTRITIONAL ANALYSIS

(figures are per sandwich)

Calories = 547
Fat = 13.9g
of which saturates = 3.7g
    monounsaturates = 4.4g
    polyunsaturates = 4.2g

Protein = 31.9g
Carbohydrate = 78.4g
Dietary fiber = 9.2g
Sodium = 1.6g

Percentage of total calories from fat = 23%, of which saturates = 6%
Percentage of total calories from carbohydrate = 54%, of which sugars = 12%

CHEESE & DATE BREAD

Preparation time: 20 minutes

Cooking time: 35-45 minutes

Makes one 1-pound loaf (10 slices)

2 cups self-rising flour
pinch of salt
$^1/_4$ cup soft margarine
$^1/_3$ cup finely shredded reduced-fat sharp Cheddar
cheese
$^1/_2$ cup dried pitted dates, finely chopped
2 eggs
$^2/_3$ cup low-fat or 2% milk

1 Sift the flour and salt into a bowl. Rub in the margarine until the mixture resembles fine bread crumbs. Add $^1/_3$ cup of the cheese and the dates and mix well.

2 Beat the eggs and milk together, add to the date mixture, and mix well. Turn the mixture into a lightly greased 1-pound loaf pan and level the surface. Sprinkle with the remaining cheese.

3 Bake in a preheated oven at 375° for 35-45 minutes, until risen and golden brown. Turn out and cool on a wire rack. Serve warm or cold in slices.

NUTRITIONAL ANALYSIS

(figures are per slice)

Calories = 192
Fat = 7.5g
of which saturates = 2.2g
    monounsaturates = 2.1g
    polyunsaturates = 2.5g
Protein = 7.0g
Carbohydrate = 25.7g
Dietary fiber = 1.2g
Sodium = 0.3g

Percentage of total calories from fat = 35%
of which saturates = 10%
Percentage of total calories from carbohydrate
= 50%, of which sugars = 17%

WHOLE-WHEAT RAISIN & ORANGE
MUFFINS

These light muffins are best served warm on their own, or spread with a small amount of low-fat spread or jelly. Try one of the variations to sample some different flavors for breakfast, brunch, or a snack. Serve the muffins with a piece of fresh fruit for a change.

1 Reserve 2 tbsp whole-wheat flour and set aside. Sift the remaining flours into a bowl with the baking powder and salt.

2 Melt the margarine and mix together with the sugar, egg, milk, and grated orange rind.

3 Pour the mixture over the dry ingredients and fold the ingredients gently together — just enough to combine the mixture. The mixture should look quite lumpy, which is correct since over-mixing will result in heavy muffins.

4 Toss the raisins in the remaining flour and fold gently into the muffin mixture.

5 Spoon the mixture into an 8- or 12-cup lightly greased muffin pan.

6 Bake in a preheated oven at 400° for 15-20 minutes, until well-risen and golden brown.

7 Allow to cool in the pan for a few minutes, then unmold onto a wire rack to cool completely.

8 Store in an airtight container at room temperature for up to 2 days. The muffins may be reheated before serving.

VARIATIONS
● Use peeled, cored, and chopped tart apples, fresh or frozen raspberries, loganberries, or blueberries in place of the raisins and orange rind.
● Add 1-2 tsp ground mixed spice, pumpkin pie spice, or cinnamon to the mixture before baking.

Preparation time: 25 minutes
Cooking time: 15-20 minutes
Makes 8 large or 12 medium-sized muffins

1 cup whole-wheat flour
1/3 cup all-purpose flour
1 tbsp baking powder
pinch of salt
1/4 cup soft margarine
2 tbsp sugar
1 egg, beaten
7/8 cup low-fat or 2% milk
finely grated rind of 1 orange
1/2 cup raisins

NUTRITIONAL ANALYSIS
(figures are per muffin) = serving 8 (making 8 large muffins)

Calories = 222	Protein = 4.9g
Fat = 7.3g	Carbohydrate = 36.4g
of which saturates = 1.7g	Dietary fiber = 1.9g
monounsaturates = 1.9g	Sodium = 0.3g
polyunsaturates = 3.1g	

Percentage of total calories from fat = 29%, of which saturates = 7%
Percentage of total calories from carbohydrate = 61%
of which sugars = 32%

FRUIT & SPICE
COFFEECAKE

This tasty coffeecake is ideal for a filling breakfast or a quick snack at any time of the day. Try toasting slices of the coffeecake for a bedtime snack.

Preparation time: 20 minutes

Cooking time: 1 hour

Makes one 2-pound loaf (12 slices)

2 cups self-rising flour
$^1/_2$ tsp baking soda
1 tbsp ground mixed spice
$^2/_3$ cup light soft brown sugar
$^1/_2$ cup yellow raisins
$^1/_2$ cup raisins
$^1/_2$ cup currants
$^1/_2$ cup finely chopped ready-to-eat dried apricots
2 eggs
$1^1/_4$ cups low-fat or 2% milk

1 Sift the flour, baking soda, and mixed spice into a bowl. Add the sugar and dried fruits, and mix well.

2 Beat the eggs and milk together and add to the fruit mixture. Beat until thoroughly mixed.

3 Turn the mixture into a lightly greased 2-pound loaf pan and level the surface.

4 Bake in a preheated oven at 350° for about 1 hour, until risen, golden brown, and firm to the touch.

5 Leave in the pan to cool for a few minutes, then transfer to a wire rack to cool completely.

6 Serve the coffeecake, warm or cold, in slices on its own. Alternatively, spread the coffeecake with a small amount of reduced-sugar jelly or jam, or honey.

VARIATIONS
● Use chopped candied cherries or candied peel in place of the currants.
● Add the finely grated rind of 1 lemon or 1 orange to the mixture before baking.

NUTRITIONAL ANALYSIS

(figures are per slice)

Calories = 209
Fat = 1.6g
of which saturates = 0.5g
    monounsaturates = 0.5g
    polyunsaturates = 0.2g

Protein = 4.4g
Carbohydrate = 47.8g
Dietary fiber = 1.8g
Sodium = 0.1g

Percentage of total calories from fat = 7%
of which saturates = 2%
Percentage of total calories from carbohydrate = 85%
of which sugars = 60%

BANANA & GINGER LOAF

The flavors of banana and ginger combine perfectly in this delicious loaf. Serve warm or cold slices on their own or with a little low-fat spread for a snack, or spread with reduced-sugar jam for a quick and tasty brunch.

Preparation time: 25 minutes

Cooking time: 1-1¼ hours

Makes one 2-pound loaf (12 slices)

½ cup soft margarine
⅔ cup light soft brown sugar
2 eggs, beaten
2 cups self-rising flour
½ tsp baking soda
pinch of salt
2 tsp ground ginger
4 large bananas
⅓ cup preserved ginger, finely chopped

1 Cream the margarine and sugar together until light and fluffy. Gradually add the eggs, beating well after each addition.

2 Sift the flour, baking soda, salt, and ginger together and fold into the creamed mixture.

3 Peel the bananas and mash the flesh. Add the banana purée to the cake mixture and beat until well mixed. Stir in the preserved ginger and mix well.

4 Turn the mixture into a lightly greased 2-pound loaf pan and level the surface.

5 Bake in a preheated oven at 350° for 1-1¼ hours, until well-risen, golden brown, and firm to the touch.

6 Allow to cool in the pan for a few minutes, then turn out onto a wire rack to cool completely.

NUTRITIONAL ANALYSIS
(figures are per slice)

Calories = 238
Fat = 9.2g
of which saturates = 1.9g
          monounsaturates = 2.4g
          polyunsaturates = 4.2g

Protein = 3.4g
Carbohydrate = 38.1g
Dietary fiber = 1.1g
Sodium = 0.2g

Percentage of total calories from fat = 35%, of which saturates = 7%
Percentage of total calories from carbohydrate = 60%
of which sugars = 36%

VARIATIONS
● Omit the ground and preserved ginger and replace with ¾ cup chopped dried fruits such as yellow raisins, peaches, or apricots.
● Use ground mixed spice in place of the ground ginger.
● Use granulated sugar in place of the brown sugar.

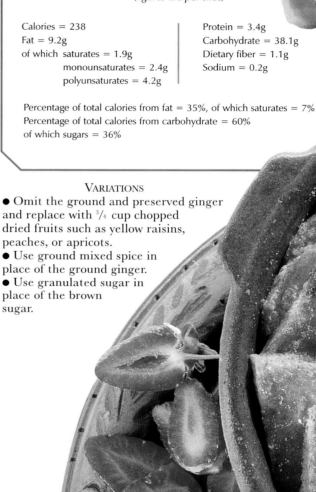

SPICED APRICOT & BREAD
LAYER DESSERT

This dessert can be served with fresh fruit, such as sliced peaches or strawberries. For a special treat, serve with reduced-fat cream.

Preparation time: 25 minutes, plus 30 minutes standing time

Cooking time: 1 hour

Serves 4

6 medium slices whole-wheat bread
2 tbsp soft margarine
3 tbsp reduced-sugar apricot jam or jelly
$1/3$ cup chopped ready-to-eat dried apricots
3 tbsp light soft brown sugar
2 tsp ground mixed spice
2 eggs
$2^1/2$ cups low-fat or 2% milk

1 Remove and discard the crusts from the bread (the crusts may be made into bread crumbs for use in another recipe). Spread the bread slices with margarine and then with jam or jelly.

2 Cut into triangles or fingers and place half in a lightly greased ovenproof dish. Sprinkle the apricots over the top.

3 Mix together the sugar and spice and sprinkle half over the apricots. Top with the remaining bread, jam side upward, and sprinkle with the remaining sugar-and-spice mixture.

4 Beat the eggs and milk together and strain into the dish over the bread. Leave to stand for 30 minutes, so that the bread absorbs most of the liquid.

5 Bake in a preheated oven at 325° for 45-60 minutes, until set and golden brown on top. Serve hot or cold.

NUTRITIONAL ANALYSIS

(figures are per serving)

Calories = 359	Protein = 14.3g
Fat = 12.1g	Carbohydrate = 52.2g
of which saturates = 3.7g	Dietary fiber = 4.4g
monounsaturates = 3.7g	Sodium = 0.5g
polyunsaturates = 3.3g	

Percentage of total calories from fat = 30%, of which saturates = 9%

Percentage of total calories from carbohydrate = 55%, of which sugars = 34%

CHAPTER TWO

CEREALS

*C*ereals such as wheat and oats form a valuable and nutritious part of our diet. Wheat (often eaten as flour) and oats (most commonly eaten as oatmeal) are a good source of carbohydrates. They are low in fat, some contain fiber, and they have many uses in cooking — in breads, cookies, biscuits, and scones.
In addition, oats contain soluble fiber, which can be helpful in lowering blood cholesterol levels if eaten as part of a low-fat diet. Some cereals, including oats and wheat, provide the basis for the wide variety of breakfast cereals available. Many breakfast cereals, including granola, are fortified with vitamins and minerals, and the whole-grain varieties are also high in fiber.

COD, CORN, & BROCCOLI
CRÊPES

*These filled crêpes are ideal for serving as a light lunch or brunch.
Serve with some fresh crusty bread or hot toast.*

Preparation time: 25 minutes

Cooking time: 20 minutes

Serves 4 (two pancakes per serving)

¹/₂ cup all-purpose flour
¹/₂ cup whole-wheat flour
pinch of salt
1 egg
1¹/₄ cups low-fat or 2% milk
1 cup small broccoli flowerets
1 tsp sunflower oil, plus extra for cooking the pancakes
1 small onion, minced
1 clove garlic, crushed
1 cup canned, peeled tomatoes, chopped
1 tbsp tomato ketchup
salt and freshly ground black pepper
1 cup cubed skinless cod fillets
³/₄ cup drained canned corn kernels
2 tbsp minced fresh coriander (cilantro)

1 Make the crêpe mixture following Steps 1 and 2 for the Orange and Cinnamon Crêpes on page 33.

2 Cook the broccoli in a saucepan of boiling water for about 5 minutes, until just cooked. Drain and keep warm.

3 Meanwhile, heat 1 tsp oil in a saucepan, add the onion and garlic, and cook gently for 5 minutes, stirring occasionally.

4 Add the tomatoes, tomato ketchup, and seasoning, mix well and bring to the boil. Add the cod and corn and stir gently to mix.

5 Cover and cook gently for about 10 minutes, stirring occasionally, until the fish is just cooked. Add the broccoli and coriander (cilantro) and stir gently to mix. Keep hot while cooking the pancakes.

6 Cook the crêpes following Steps 4 and 5 for the Orange and Cinnamon Crêpes on page 33.

7 Place some filling onto one half of a crêpe. Fold the other half over the filling, then fold in half again to form a triangle.

The filling for these crêpes can be cooked in a microwave oven.

26

NUTRITIONAL ANALYSIS

(figures are per serving)

Calories = 299
Fat = 6.9g
of which saturates = 1.8g
    monounsaturates = 1.8g
    polyunsaturates = 2.4g
Protein = 21.7g
Carbohydrate = 40.0g
Dietary fiber = 4.1g
Sodium = 0.5g

Percentage of total calories from fat = 21%
of which saturates = 5%
Percentage of total calories from carbohydrate
= 50%, of which sugars = 16%

CHEESE & PEAR
SCONES

Dried fruits — pears in this case — combine well with cheese and make these scones full of flavor. Serve them freshly baked, warm or cold, with your favorite spread or preserve.

Preparation time: 20 minutes
Cooking time: 10 minutes
Makes about 16 scones

1½ cups all-purpose whole-wheat flour
½ cup graham flour
pinch of salt
2 tsp baking powder
3 tbsp soft margarine
½ cup finely shredded, reduced-fat sharp Cheddar cheese
⅔ cup finely chopped ready-to-eat dried pears
⅔ cup low-fat or 2% milk, plus extra for glazing

1 Mix the flour, graham flour, salt, and baking powder in a bowl, then rub in the margarine until the mixture resembles bread crumbs.

2 Stir in all but 1 tbsp of the cheese and the pears and mix well. Add enough milk to form a soft but not sticky dough.

3 Turn onto a lightly floured surface and knead very lightly.

Roll or pat the dough out lightly until about ¾ inch thick. Using a 2-inch plain cookie cutter, cut the dough into approximately 16 rounds.

4 Place on lightly floured baking sheets. Brush the tops with milk and sprinkle with the remaining cheese.

5 Bake in a preheated oven at 425° for about 10 minutes, until risen and golden brown. Transfer to a wire rack to cool. Serve warm or cold.

VARIATIONS

● Use other dried fruits, such as apples or apricots, in place of the pears.
● Use other reduced-fat hard cheese such as Monterey jack in place of the Cheddar.
● Use white all-purpose flour or a mixture of white and whole-wheat in place of the whole-wheat flour.

NUTRITIONAL ANALYSIS

(figures are per scone)

Calories = 107
Fat = 3.9g
of which saturates = 1.3g
    monounsaturates = 1.0g
    polyunsaturates = 1.3g

Protein = 4.5g
Carbohydrate = 14.5g
Dietary fiber = 1.9g
Sodium = 0.2g

Percentage of total calories from fat = 32%, of which saturates = 10%
Percentage of total calories from carbohydrate = 51%, of which sugars = 19%

RAISIN & LEMON COOKIES

These crumbly, melt-in-the-mouth cookies are an ideal treat to enjoy as a snack with coffee or tea. Once you have tasted one of these delicious cookies, you'll find it hard to resist eating more!

Preparation time: 15 minutes
Cooking time: 15-20 minutes
Makes about 18 cookies

$^1/_2$ *cup soft margarine*
$^1/_2$ *cup sugar*
finely grated rind of 1 lemon
1 egg, beaten
1$^1/_2$ cups all-purpose flour
2 tsp baking powder
pinch of salt
4 tbsp raw medium oatmeal
1 cup raisins

1 Cream the margarine, sugar, and lemon rind together until pale and fluffy. Gradually add the egg, beating well after each addition.

2 Sift the flour, baking powder, and salt together and add to the creamed mixture with the raw oatmeal, mixing well. Add the raisins and mix well.

3 Place heaping teaspoons of the mixture onto two lightly greased baking sheets and flatten them slightly with the back of a fork.

4 Bake in a preheated oven at 375° for 15-20 minutes, until golden brown. Allow to cool for a couple of minutes, then transfer to a wire rack.

VARIATIONS
● Add 1 tsp ground mixed spice to the mixture before baking.
● Use other dried fruits such as chopped apricots in place of the raisins.

NUTRITIONAL ANALYSIS
(figures are per cookie)

Calories = 156
Fat = 6.0g
of which saturates = 1.2g
    monounsaturates = 1.6g
    polyunsaturates = 2.8g

Protein = 1.9g
Carbohydrate = 25.1g
Dietary fiber = 0.8g
Sodium = 0.1g

Percentage of total calories from fat = 35%, of which saturates = 7%
Percentage of total calories from carbohydrate = 60%
of which sugars = 37%

28

PINEAPPLE BRAN
MUFFINS

These light muffins make a tempting snack at any time of the day, freshly baked on their own, or spread with a little low-fat spread or preserve.

Preparation time: 25 minutes
Cooking time: 15-20 minutes
Makes 8 large or 12 medium-sized muffins

1¹/₄ cups all-purpose flour
1 tbsp baking powder
pinch of salt
4 tbsp bran
4 tbsp soft margarine
4 tbsp light soft brown sugar
1 egg, beaten
⁷/₈ cup low-fat or 2% milk
¹/₂ cup finely chopped dried pineapple

1 Reserve 2 tbsp flour and set aside. Sift the remaining flour into a bowl with the baking powder and salt. Stir in the bran.

2 Melt the margarine and mix with the sugar, egg, and milk.

3 Pour the mixture over the dry ingredients and fold in, just enough to combine the mixture. The mixture should look quite lumpy, which is correct since over-mixing will result in heavy muffins.

4 Add the pineapple to the remaining flour and fold gently into the muffin mixture.

5 Spoon the mixture into a 8- or 12-cup lightly greased muffin pan.

6 Bake in a preheated oven at 400° for 15-20 minutes, until well-risen and golden brown.

7 Allow to cool in the pan for a few minutes, then unmold onto a wire rack to cool completely.

8 Store the muffins in an airtight container at room temperature for up to 2 days.

VARIATIONS
● Use other dried fruits such as peaches, apricots, pears, raisins, or yellow raisins in place of the pineapple.
● Use granulated sugar in place of the soft brown sugar.

NUTRITIONAL ANALYSIS

(figures are per muffin) = serving 8 (making 8 large muffins)

Calories = 213
Fat = 7.6g
of which saturates = 1.7g
    monounsaturates = 1.9g
    polyunsaturates = 3.2g

Protein = 4.8g
Carbohydrate = 33.9g
Dietary fiber = 4.2g
Sodium = 0.3g

Percentage of total calories form fat = 32%
of which saturates = 7%
Percentage of total calories from carbohydrate = 60%
of which sugars = 33%

FRUIT
BARS

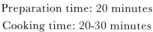

Preparation time: 20 minutes
Cooking time: 20-30 minutes
Makes 10 bars

¹/₂ cup low-fat spread
¹/₃ cup light soft brown sugar
2 tbsp dark corn syrup
2 tbsp molasses
1¹/₄ cups fine raw oatmeal
³/₄ cup medium oatmeal
1 tsp ground cinnamon
2 tbsp ready-to-eat dried apricots, finely chopped
2 tbsp ready-to-eat dried pitted dates, finely chopped

1 Place the low-fat spread, sugar, syrup, and molasses in a saucepan and heat gently, stirring, until melted.

2 Remove from the heat, add the remaining ingredients, and mix well.

3 Turn the mixture into a lightly greased, shallow 7-inch square cake pan.

4 Bake in a preheated oven at 350° for 20-30 minutes, until lightly browned.

5 Allow to cool slightly, then mark into bars. When firm, remove from the pan, break into bars, and cool on a wire rack.

NUTRITIONAL ANALYSIS

(figures are per bar)

Calories = 207

Fat = 6.5g
of which saturates = 1.5g
    monounsaturates = 0.3g
    polyunsaturates = 1.6g

Protein = 3.8g
Carbohydrate = 35.3g
Dietary fiber = 1.2g
Sodium = 0.03g

Percentage of total calories from fat = 28%
of which saturates = 7%
Percentage of total calories from carbohydrate = 64%, of which sugars = 38%

CORN, LEEK, & MUSHROOM
PIZZA

This pizza has a crispy bread base, topped with lots of tasty, nutritious vegetables — ideal for serving as a filling lunch, or as a main course meal with a large green salad.

Preparation time: 45 minutes, plus kneading and rising time for the pizza dough

Cooking time: 30-40 minutes

Makes one 10-inch pizza

FOR THE PIZZA BASE
1 tbsp fresh yeast or 1 envelope active dry yeast
1/2 tsp sugar
1 1/4 cups lukewarm water
1 cup all-purpose flour
1 cup whole-wheat flour
1/2 tsp salt
1 tbsp olive oil

FOR THE TOMATO SAUCE
14-ounce can peeled, chopped tomatoes
1 small onion, minced
1 clove garlic, crushed
1 tbsp tomato paste
1 tbsp minced fresh mixed herbs or 1 tsp dried herbs
pinch of sugar
salt and freshly ground black pepper

FOR THE TOPPING
2 tbsp minced fresh tarragon or 2 tsp dried tarragon
1 tsp olive oil
1 cup trimmed, washed, and sliced leeks
1 1/4 cups sliced mushrooms
1 1/4 cups canned corn kernels
1/2 cup finely shredded Monterey jack cheese, finely grated

1 To make the pizza base, blend fresh yeast with the sugar and water and set aside in a warm place until frothy. If using dry yeast, mix the sugar with the water, sprinkle the yeast over the water, then set aside until frothy.

2 In a bowl, stir together the flours and salt. Make a well in the center and add the yeast liquid and oil. Mix the flour into the liquid to make a firm dough.

3 Turn the dough out onto a lightly floured surface and knead for about 10 minutes, until the dough feels smooth and elastic, and is no longer sticky.

4 Place the dough in a clean bowl, cover with plastic wrap or a clean kitchen towel, and leave in a warm place until doubled in size — about 45 minutes.

5 Meanwhile, make the tomato sauce. Place the tomatoes, onion, garlic, tomato paste, herbs, sugar, and seasonings in a saucepan and mix well. Bring to the boil, then simmer, uncovered, for 15-20 minutes, until the sauce becomes fairly thick, stirring occasionally. Adjust the seasoning and set aside.

6 Turn the pizza dough out onto a lightly floured surface and knead again for 2-3 minutes.

7 Roll the dough out to a circle roughly 10 inches in diameter. Place on a baking sheet, making the edges of the dough slightly thicker than the center.

8 For the topping, spread the tomato sauce evenly over the pizza base and sprinkle the tarragon over the top. Heat the oil in a saucepan, add the leeks and mushrooms, cover, and cook gently for 10 minutes, stirring occasionally.

9 Add the corn, mix well, then spoon the mixture over the tomato sauce. Sprinkle the cheese over the pizza.

10 Bake in a preheated oven at 425° for 30-40 minutes, until the dough is risen and golden brown.

11 Serve the pizza hot or cold in slices, with a tossed green salad or homemade low-calorie coleslaw and fresh crusty bread or a baked potato.

VARIATIONS
● Use chopped cooked chicken or turkey in place of the mushrooms.
● Use other herbs such as mixed herbs or coriander (cilantro) in place of the tarragon.
● Use one large onion in place of the leeks.

NUTRITIONAL ANALYSIS
(figures are per serving of a 6-slice pizza)

Calories = 278
Fat = 6.7g
of which saturates = 2.4g
　　　　　monounsaturates = 2.6g
　　　　　polyunsaturates = 1.0g
Protein = 13.9g
Carbohydrate = 43.4g
Dietary fiber = 3.6g
Sodium = 0.4g

Percentage of total calories from fat = 21%
of which saturates = 7%
Percentage of total calories from
carbohydrate = 58%
of which sugars = 11%

PEACH & LEMON
CHEESECAKE

*This irresistible cheesecake combines a crunchy granola base with a creamy,
fruity topping — bound to satisfy those sweet tastebuds every time.*

Preparation time: 30 minutes, plus chilling time

Serves 8

*²/₃ cup dark corn syrup
1 cup unsweetened granola
14-ounce can peaches in fruit juice
1 tbsp powdered gelatin
1¹/₄ cups cottage cheese, sieved
finely grated rind and juice of 1 lemon
1¹/₄ cups reduced-fat light cream
²/₃ cup reduced-fat sour cream
2 tbsp sugar
peach slices and mint sprigs,
to decorate*

1 Pour the corn syrup in a
saucepan and heat gently
until hot but not
boiling, stirring.

2 Remove from the
heat and stir in the
granola. Spread the
mixture evenly over
the base of an 8-inch
loose-bottomed cake pan
or springform pan. Chill in
the refrigerator while making the
filling. When the base is chilled and
firm, press it down to level the surface.

3 Drain the peaches, reserving the juice
and fruit. Pour the peach juice into a
small bowl and sprinkle it with the
gelatin. Leave to soak for a few minutes,
then place the bowl
over a pan of
simmering water.
Stir until the
gelatin has dissolved.
Set aside to cool.

4 Place the peaches, cottage
cheese, lemon rind and juice, cream,
sour cream, and sugar in a blender or
food processor and blend until smooth

and thoroughly mixed. Add the cooled gelatin and blend until well mixed.

5 Pour the peach mixture over the granola base and chill in the refrigerator for several hours until set.

6 To serve, carefully remove the cheesecake from the pan and place it on a serving platter. Decorate with fresh peach slices and mint sprigs before serving.

The syrup can be heated and the gelatin can be dissolved in a microwave oven.

VARIATIONS

● Use other canned fruits such as apricots, pears, cherries, or raspberries in place of the peaches.
● Use crushed reduced-fat graham crackers, mixed grain cereal, or cornflakes in place of the granola.

NUTRITIONAL ANALYSIS

(figures are per serving)

Calories = 261
Fat = 5.7g
of which saturates = 3.2g
 monounsaturates = 1.4g
 polyunsaturates = 0.6g
Protein = 10.3g
Carbohydrate = 44.6g
Dietary fiber = 2.2g
Sodium = 0.2g

Percentage of total calories from fat = 20%
of which saturates = 10%
Percentage of total calories from carbohydrate = 64%, of which sugars = 46%

ORANGE & CINNAMON
CRÊPES

The addition of cinnamon brings extra flavor to these light and crispy crêpes. Served with the yellow raisin and orange sauce, they will provide a satisfying conclusion to any meal.

Preparation time: 25 minutes
Cooking time: 20 minutes
Serves 4 (2 crêpes per serving)

1 cup all-purpose flour
pinch of salt
1 tbsp ground cinnamon
1 egg
1 1/4 cups low-fat or 2% milk
2 tsp sunflower oil
1 1/4 cups unsweetened orange juice
1 cup yellow raisins

1 To make the crêpes, sift the flour, salt, and cinnamon into a bowl and make a well in the center. Break in the egg and add a little milk, beating well with a wooden spoon.

2 Gradually beat in the remaining milk, drawing the flour in from the sides to make a smooth mixture. Cover and set aside while making the sauce.

3 To make the sauce, place the orange juice and yellow raisins in a saucepan and stir to mix. Bring to the boil and cook gently for about 15 minutes, stirring occasionally, until most of the liquid has evaporated and the yellow raisins have plumped up.

4 Meanwhile, cook the crêpes. Brush a heavy-based 7-inch nonstick skillet with a little oil and heat until hot. Beat the mixture to ensure it is well mixed, then pour in enough to thinly coat the pan base.

5 Cook until golden brown, then turn and cook on the other side. Transfer the crêpe to a warmed plate and keep hot. Repeat with the remaining mixture to make 8 crêpes. Arrange the cooked crêpes on top of one another with a sheet of parchment paper in between each crêpe.

6 Spoon some raisin and orange sauce over each crêpe, roll the crêpes up, and serve immediately.

NUTRITIONAL ANALYSIS

(figures are per serving)

Calories = 350
Fat = 5.0g
of which saturates = 1.5g
 monounsaturates = 1.4g
 polyunsaturates = 1.3g
Protein = 8.9g
Carbohydrate = 71.9g
Dietary fiber = 2.1g
Sodium = 0.3g

Percentage of total calories from fat = 13%
of which saturates = 4%
Percentage of total calories from carbohydrate = 77%, of which sugars = 54%

CHAPTER THREE

PASTA

*P*asta is an essential item in every kitchen, and is an excellent basis for many quick and tasty meals. There are two main types of pasta: egg pasta and eggless pasta. Both are available fresh or dried, and homemade pasta is also a popular choice. Filled pasta shapes such as tortellini and ravioli are also available in fresh and dried forms.

There are many shapes of pasta to choose from, as well as a range of different flavors, including spinach, tomato, chili, herb, or black squid ink. Pasta is naturally high in carbohydrates and low in fat. Whole-wheat varieties also contain fiber and some B vitamins. Avoid high-fat pasta sauces, especially the cream-based varieties. Tomato-based sauces tend to be much lower in fat and are just as flavorsome.

PASTA TWISTS WITH SMOKED HAM & TOMATO SAUCE

Fresh tomatoes always provide a good basis for a pasta sauce. They combine particularly well with mushrooms and smoked ham in this recipe to create a nutritious and filling meal.

Preparation time: 15 minutes
Cooking time: 20 minutes
Serves 4

4¹/₂ cups tomatoes, skinned and chopped
1 large onion, chopped
2 cloves garlic, crushed
1³/₄ cups button mushrooms, halved
1 tbsp tomato ketchup
1 tbsp tomato paste
salt and freshly ground black pepper
6 ounces cooked lean smoked ham, diced
1 pound pasta twists
2 tbsp chopped fresh mixed herbs
fresh Parmesan cheese shavings, to serve

1 Place the tomatoes, onion, garlic, mushrooms, tomato ketchup, tomato paste, and seasoning in a saucepan and mix well.

2 Cover, bring to the boil, then simmer gently for 15-20 minutes, stirring occasionally, until the vegetables are tender. Stir in the ham and cook gently for 5 minutes.

3 Meanwhile, cook the pasta in a large saucepan of lightly salted, boiling water for 10-12 minutes, until just cooked or *al dente*.

4 Drain the pasta thoroughly and toss it with the tomato sauce and fresh herbs, or spoon the sauce over the pasta. Serve immediately, sprinkled with some shavings of fresh Parmesan cheese. Serve with fresh crusty bread rolls and a mixed green salad.

The pasta sauce is suitable for freezing, and can also be cooked in a microwave oven.

VARIATIONS
● Use unsmoked ham or cooked chicken in place of the smoked ham.
● Use two 14-ounce cans peeled, chopped tomatoes in place of the fresh tomatoes.

WHOLE-WHEAT SPAGHETTI WITH COUNTRY-STYLE CHICKEN SAUCE

Preparation time: 20 minutes

Cooking time: 1 hour

Serves 4

2 tsp olive oil
1 onion, sliced
1 clove garlic, crushed
1¹/₂ cups skinless, boneless chicken breast, diced
3 slices smoked lean back bacon, diced
1 green bell pepper, seeded and sliced
1¹/₂ cups sliced carrots
1¹/₄ cups sliced mushrooms
2¹/₂ cups chicken broth
2 tbsp dry sherry
2 tbsp tomato paste
2 tsp dried mixed herbs
salt and freshly ground black pepper
2 tbsp cornstarch
1 pound whole-wheat spaghetti
chopped fresh parsley to garnish

1 Heat the oil in a large saucepan and cook the onion, garlic, and chicken for 5 minutes, stirring occasionally. Add the bacon, green bell pepper, carrots, and mushrooms and mix well.

2 Combine the broth, sherry, tomato paste, herbs, and seasoning and add to the pan, mixing well. Cover, bring to the boil, then simmer for 45-60 minutes, stirring occasionally, until the chicken is cooked and the vegetables are tender.

3 Blend the cornstarch with 3 tbsp water and stir into the chicken sauce. Bring back to the boil, stirring continuously, then simmer for 3 minutes, stirring.

4 Meanwhile, cook the pasta in a large saucepan of lightly salted, boiling water for 10-12 minutes, until the pasta is just cooked or *al dente*.

5 Drain the pasta thoroughly and serve it with the chicken sauce spooned over the top. Garnish with chopped fresh parsley. Serve with fresh crusty bread.

VARIATION
● Use tomato sauce in place of the tomato paste.

PASTA SHELLS WITH
SMOKED FISH,
SHRIMP, & GARDEN PEAS

NUTRITIONAL ANALYSIS
(figures are per serving)

Calories = 639
Fat = 15.3g
of which saturates = 4.2g
    monounsaturates = 3.5g
    polyunsaturates = 6.0g
Protein = 42.7g
Carbohydrate = 88.1g
Dietary fiber = 9.3g
Sodium = 1.2g

Percentage of total calories from fat = 22%
of which saturates = 6%
Percentage of total calories from
carbohydrate = 52%, of which sugars = 10%
Good source of calcium

Serve this sumptuous pasta dish, rich in flavor, texture, and color, with some warm, crusty whole-wheat bread. Choose other types of pasta, such as fettuccine or pasta twists, for variety.

Preparation time: 15 minutes

Cooking time: 25 minutes

Serves 4

6 ounces skinless smoked cod
or white fish fillet
1 bay leaf
6 black peppercorns
1 stick celery, chopped
3 cups low-fat or 2% milk
1¼ cups broccoli flowerets
¾ cup cauliflower flowerets
1¼ cups frozen garden peas
3 tbsp soft margarine
1 red onion, chopped
3 tbsp all-purpose flour
8 cooked jumbo shrimp, deveined and shelled
2 tbsp minced fresh coriander (cilantro) (optional)
salt and freshly ground black pepper
1 pound pasta shells

1 Place the smoked fish in a saucepan with the bay leaf, peppercorns, and celery. Add the milk, cover, and heat gently until almost boiling. Simmer for 7-10 minutes, until the fish is just cooked. Remove the fish from the pan using a slotted spoon and keep warm.

2 Strain and reserve the milk, and discard the flavorings. Cook the broccoli, cauliflower, and garden peas in boiling water for 5 minutes, until just tender. Drain and keep warm.

3 Meanwhile, melt the margarine in a large saucepan and cook the onion for 5 minutes, stirring. Add the flour and cook gently for 1 minute, stirring. Remove the pan from the heat and gradually stir in the milk.

4 Heat gently, stirring continuously, until the sauce comes to the boil and thickens. Simmer gently for 3 minutes, stirring.

5 Flake the cooked fish and add to the sauce with the cooked vegetables, shrimp, coriander (cilantro), if using, and seasoning, and mix well. Reheat gently until the sauce is piping hot.

6 Meanwhile, cook the pasta in a large saucepan of lightly salted, boiling water for 10-12 minutes, until just cooked or *al dente*.

7 Drain the pasta thoroughly and serve immediately with the sauce spooned over the top, or tossed with the pasta.

VARIATION
● Use 1 cup cooked, shelled, and deveined bay shrimp or cooked, shelled mussels in place of the jumbo shrimp.

MEDITERRANEAN
PASTA MEDLEY
WITH TUNA & CORN

Some of the typical flavors of the Mediterranean are brought together in this pasta sauce to create a delectable entrée — perfect to enjoy in the evening or at midday alfresco.

Preparation time: 15 minutes

Cooking time: 25 minutes

Serves 4

*14-ounce can peeled
chopped tomatoes
1 onion, minced
1 clove garlic, crushed
1 red bell pepper, seeded and cut into large dice
2 cups sliced zucchini
1 cup minced celery
²/₃ cup dry white wine
1 tbsp tomato paste
14-ounce can tuna in water, drained and flaked
2 cups corn kernels, drained
2 tbsp chopped fresh basil
1 tbsp chopped fresh parsley
salt and freshly ground black pepper
1 pound penne noodles*

1 Place the tomatoes, onion, garlic, pepper, zucchini, celery, wine, and tomato paste in a saucepan and mix well. Cover, bring to the boil, and simmer for about 10 minutes, stirring occasionally. Uncover the pan and cook for a further 5 minutes, stirring occasionally.

2 Add the tuna, corn, herbs, and seasoning and stir to mix. Reheat gently for about 5 minutes, until the sauce is piping hot.

3 Meanwhile, cook the pasta in a large saucepan of lightly salted, boiling water for 10-12 minutes, until just cooked or *al dente*.

4 Drain the pasta thoroughly, toss with the tuna sauce, and serve immediately with some fresh, crusty French bread or warm multi-grain rolls and a mixed leaf salad.

VARIATIONS
● Use other canned fish such as salmon in place of the tuna.
● Use 2 cups sliced mushrooms in place of the corn.
● Use red wine in place of the white wine, or grape juice.
● Use chopped fresh mixed herbs in place of the basil and parsley.

NUTRITIONAL ANALYSIS
(figures are per serving)

Calories = 565
Fat = 4.2g
of which saturates = 0.7g
monounsaturates = 0.6g
polyunsaturates = 1.7g
Protein = 34.3g
Carbohydrate = 97.7g
Dietary fiber = 7.6g
Sodium = 0.6g

Percentage of total calories from fat = 7%
of which saturates = 1%
Percentage of total calories from
carbohydrate = 65%
of which sugars = 13%

FETTUCCINE
WITH SPINACH & BLUE CHEESE SAUCE

Preparation time: 15 minutes

Cooking time: 15 minutes

Serves 4

1 pound fettuccine
2 tbsp soft margarine
1 clove garlic, crushed
4 shallots, finely chopped
2 tbsp all-purpose flour
2 cups low-fat or 2% milk
3 cups cooked, drained spinach
1/3 cup blue cheese, crumbled
salt and freshly ground black pepper
minced fresh parsley, to garnish

1 Cook the pasta in a large saucepan of lightly salted, boiling water for 10-12 minutes, until just cooked or *al dente*.

2 Meanwhile, make the spinach and blue cheese sauce. Melt the margarine in a saucepan, add the garlic and shallots, and cook gently for 5 minutes, stirring.

3 Add the flour and cook for 1 minute, stirring. Remove the pan from the heat and gradually stir in the milk.

4 Heat gently, stirring continuously, until the sauce comes to the boil and thickens. Reduce the heat and simmer gently for 3 minutes, stirring.

5 Press any excess water out of the spinach using the back of a wooden spoon, then chop the spinach.

6 Add the spinach, cheese, and seasoning to the sauce and mix well. Reheat gently, stirring continuously, until the cheese has melted and the sauce is piping hot.

7 Drain the cooked pasta thoroughly, then toss it with the sauce and serve immediately, garnished with some minced parsley. Alternatively, serve the pasta with the sauce spooned over it. Serve this dish with crusty bread rolls and a mixed leaf salad.

VARIATIONS
● Use other types of pasta such as whole-wheat spaghetti or pasta shapes in place of the fettuccine.
● Use 1 small standard or red onion or 1 bunch of green onions (scallions) in place of the shallots.
● Use a sharp yellow cheese instead of blue cheese.
● Add 1/3 cup diced lean ham or cooked bacon to the sauce before serving.

NUTRITIONAL ANALYSIS
(figures are per serving)

Calories = 527
Fat = 15.7g
of which saturates = 6.2g
      monounsaturates = 3.9g
      polyunsaturates = 4.2g
Protein = 22.7g
Carbohydrate = 78.6g
Dietary fiber = 5.9g
Sodium = 0.4g

Percentage of total calories from fat = 27%
of which saturates = 10%
Percentage of total calories from carbohydrate = 56%
of which sugars = 7%s
Good source of calcium & vitamin A

SPAGHETTI
WITH MIXED
VEGETABLES

Preparation time: 15 minutes

Cooking time: 25 minutes

Serves 4

2 tsp olive oil
1 red onion, sliced
2 cloves garlic, crushed
14-ounce can peeled, chopped tomatoes
1-pound can chick-peas (garbanzo beans), rinsed
and drained
1 cup sliced zucchini
1 cup baby corn, halved
³/₄ cup okra, trimmed
²/₃ cup tomato sauce
2 tbsp red wine
1 tbsp tomato paste
1 tsp sugar
2 tsp dried mixed herbs
salt and freshly ground black pepper
1 pound tricolor spaghetti
1 cup cherry tomatoes, halved
chopped fresh parsley, to garnish

1 Heat the oil in a saucepan, add the onion and garlic, and cook for 5 minutes, stirring occasionally. Add the tomatoes, chick-peas (garbanzo beans), zucchini, corn, okra, tomato sauce, wine, tomato paste, sugar, herbs, and seasoning and mix well.

2 Cover, bring to the boil, and simmer for 15-20 minutes, stirring occasionally.

3 Meanwhile, cook the pasta in a large saucepan of lightly salted, boiling water for 10-12 minutes, until just cooked or *al dente*.

4 Drain the pasta thoroughly. Stir the cherry tomatoes into the vegetable sauce. Toss the pasta with the vegetable sauce and serve immediately, sprinkled with fresh parsley. Serve with crusty bread rolls and a green side salad.

The mixed vegetable pasta sauce can be cooked in a microwave oven.

NUTRITIONAL ANALYSIS
(figures are per serving)

Calories = 482
Fat = 6.7g
of which saturates = 0.9g
   monounsaturates = 1.9g
   polyunsaturates = 2.3g
Protein = 20.8g
Carbohydrate = 88.8g
Dietary fiber = 10.7g
Sodium = 0.7g

Percentage of total calories
from fat = 12%
of which saturates = 2%
Percentage of total calories
from carbohydrate = 69%
of which sugars = 11%

QUICK & EASY
VEGETARIAN PASTA SAUCES

CHEDDAR & LEEK
Follow the recipe for Fettucine with Spinach & Blue Cheese Sauce on page 38 but replace the blue cheese with ¹/₂ cup grated sharp Cheddar cheese and the spinach with 2 cups sliced steamed leeks. Add 1 tbsp chopped fresh tarragon to the sauce for extra flavor.

MUSHROOM & ZUCCHINI
Alternatively, follow the recipe on page 38, replacing the shallots with 1 onion. Use 1 cup sliced, sautéed mushrooms and 1 cup sliced, sautéed zucchini in place of the spinach and use grated Monterey jack cheese in place of the blue cheese.

CHILI &
MACARONI BAKE

This macaroni bake makes a tasty entrée for serving at lunchtime or in the evening. Serve with a crisp green salad and fresh crusty French bread.

Preparation time: 1½ hours
Cooking time: 25-30 minutes
Serves 6

NUTRITIONAL ANALYSIS
(figures are per serving)

Calories = 415
Fat = 9.9g
of which saturates = 4.2g
     monounsaturates = 2.5g
     polyunsaturates = 1.3g
Protein = 25.3g
Carbohydrate = 55.4g
Dietary fiber = 6.7g
Sodium = 0.4g

Percentage of total calories from fat = 21%
of which saturates = 9%
Percentage of total calories from
carbohydrate = 50%
of which sugars = 13%
Good source of vitamin
A & B vitamins

8 ounces extra-lean ground beef
1 onion, minced
1 clove garlic, crushed
³/₄ cup finely diced carrots
³/₄ cup finely chopped mushrooms
1 small red bell pepper, seeded and finely diced
2 small fresh red chilies, seeded and finely chopped
1 cup canned peeled, chopped tomatoes
²/₃ cup red wine
²/₃ cup tomato sauce
1 tsp dried mixed herbs
salt and freshly ground black pepper
1 pound canned red kidney beans, rinsed and drained
12 ounces short-cut macaroni
2 tbsp low-fat spread
2 tbsp all-purpose flour
2½ cups low-fat or 2% milk
4 tbsp finely grated reduced-fat sharp Cheddar cheese
2 tbsp fresh whole-wheat bread crumbs

1 To make the chili, place the ground beef, onion, and garlic in a saucepan and cook gently until the meat is browned all over.

2 Add the carrots, mushrooms, red bell pepper, chilies, tomatoes, red wine, tomato sauce, herbs, and seasoning, and mix well. Cover, bring to the boil, and simmer for 30 minutes, stirring occasionally.

3 Add the kidney beans and mix well. Cover and cook for a further 15 minutes, stirring occasionally.

4 Meanwhile, cook the macaroni in a large saucepan of lightly salted, boiling water for about 10 minutes, until just cooked, then drain thoroughly and keep warm.

5 Place the low-fat spread, flour, and milk in a saucepan and heat gently, whisking continuously, until the sauce comes to the boil and thickens. Simmer gently for 3 minutes, whisking, then season with salt and pepper.

6 Mix together the chili and cooked macaroni and transfer to an ovenproof dish. Pour the white sauce over the top. Mix the cheese and bread crumbs together and sprinkle them over the chili.

7 Bake in a preheated oven at 350° for 25-30 minutes, until golden and bubbling. Serve immediately.

VARIATIONS
● Use ground soya protein or other lean ground meats such as pork or turkey in place of the beef.
● Use dry white wine in place of the red wine.
● Use other reduced-fat hard cheese such as Monterey jack in place of the Cheddar cheese.
● Use one tsp dried chili flakes in place of the fresh red chilies.

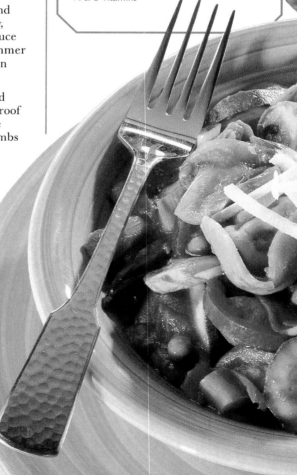

TORTELLINI PRIMAVERA

Filled pasta is often served on its own or tossed in melted butter or oil. Try this hearty and flavorful alternative, consisting of tortellini tossed with a mixture of colorful vegetables combined to make an exciting sauce.

Preparation time: 15 minutes

Cooking time: 25 minutes

Serves 4

14-ounce can peeled, chopped tomatoes
²/₃ cup tomato sauce
6 shallots, sliced
1 clove garlic, crushed
1¹/₄ cups sliced mushrooms
1¹/₄ cups sliced zucchini
1 red bell pepper, seeded and sliced into strips
8 canned asparagus spears, chopped
2 tbsp sun-dried tomatoes, finely chopped
1 bay leaf
salt and freshly ground black pepper
¹/₂ cup frozen peas
1 pound meat-filled tortellini
2-3 tbsp chopped fresh mixed herbs
4 tbsp finely grated fresh Parmesan cheese, to serve
fresh basil sprigs, to garnish

1 Place the canned tomatoes, tomato sauce, shallots, garlic, mushrooms, zucchini, bell pepper, asparagus, sun-dried tomatoes, bay leaf, and seasoning in a saucepan and mix well.

2 Cover, bring to the boil, and simmer gently for 15 minutes, stirring occasionally. Remove the bay leaf, stir in the peas, and cook for a further 5 minutes, stirring occasionally.

3 Meanwhile, cook the tortellini in a large saucepan of lightly salted, boiling water for 16-18 minutes (or according to the manufacturer's instructions), until cooked and tender.

4 Drain the pasta thoroughly. Toss the tortellini with the sauce and herbs, and sprinkle with Parmesan cheese. Garnish with fresh basil sprigs and serve with fresh crusty bread.

VARIATIONS
● Use cheese-filled tortellini in place of the meat-filled tortellini.
● Use frozen lima beans in place of the peas.
● Use 4 large skinned and chopped fresh tomatoes in place of the canned tomatoes.
● Use baby corn in place of the asparagus.
● Use reduced-fat Cheddar cheese in place of the Parmesan.

NUTRITIONAL ANALYSIS

(figures are per serving)

Calories = 502
Fat = 12.9g
of which saturates = 5.6g
monounsaturates = 4.3g
polyunsaturates = 2.0g
Protein = 28.4g
Carbohydrate = 68.5g
Dietary fiber = 7.8g
Sodium = 0.6g

Percentage of total calories from fat = 23%
of which saturates = 10%
Percentage of total calories from
carbohydrate = 51%
of which sugars = 8%
Good source of vitamins A & C

41

FUSILLI SALAD

The dressing in this recipe, with a refreshing hint of horseradish, combines well with the pasta and vegetables to make an attractive and nutritious salad, ideal as a entrée or a filling evening snack.

Preparation time: 15 minutes
Cooking time: 10-12 minutes
Serves 4

14 ounces tricolor fusilli or spiral pasta
5 tsp olive oil
4 shallots, sliced
2 cloves garlic, crushed
2 cups zucchini, cut into matchstick strips
2 cups fresh wild mushrooms such as oyster or shiitake
1 tbsp pitted black olives, finely chopped (optional)
²/₃ cup reduced-fat sour cream
²/₃ cup low-fat plain yogurt
2 tbsp horseradish sauce
salt and freshly ground black pepper
2 tbsp chopped fresh mixed herbs

1 Cook the pasta in a large saucepan of lightly salted, boiling water for 10-12 minutes, until just cooked or *al dente.*

2 Meanwhile, heat the oil in a saucepan, add the shallots, and garlic, and cook for 3 minutes, stirring occasionally. Add the zucchini and mushrooms, mix well, cover, and cook for 5 minutes, stirring occasionally. Add the olives, if using, and mix well.

3 In a bowl, mix together the sour cream, yogurt, horseradish sauce, seasoning, and herbs.

4 Drain the pasta thoroughly, then toss together with the mushroom mixture.

5 Toss the pasta and sour cream mixtures together and serve warm or cold with thick slices of fresh whole-wheat bread.

NUTRITIONAL ANALYSIS
(figures are per serving)

Calories = 426
Fat = 13.6g
of which saturates = 5.1g
   monounsaturates = 5.1g
   polyunsaturates = 2.0g

Protein = 15.7g
Carbohydrate = 63.9g
Dietary fiber = 5.4
Sodium = 0.2g

Percentage of total calories from fat = 29%
of which saturates = 10%
Percentage of total calories from carbohydrate = 56%
of which sugars = 8%

VARIATIONS
● Use 1 small onion in place of the shallots.
● Use button or closed cup mushrooms in place of the wild mushrooms.
● Use a flavored oil such as chili or herb oil in place of the olive oil.

BELL PEPPER, TOMATO, & SPINACH
PASTA SALAD

This colorful salad is tossed with a delicious mustard and herb-flavored dressing. Serve warm for a brunch or a light evening meal, or make it in advance and pack it up for a tasty brown bag lunch.

Preparation time: 15 minutes

Cooking time: 10-12 minutes

Serves 4

12 ounces pasta shapes
5 tbsp olive oil
2 tbsp red wine vinegar
2 tsp whole-grain mustard
1 clove garlic, crushed
1 tbsp chopped fresh basil
1 tbsp chopped fresh oregano
salt and freshly ground black pepper
1 red bell pepper, seeded and diced
1 yellow bell pepper, seeded and diced
1¹/₂ cups cherry tomatoes, halved
1 cup fresh baby spinach leaves, washed and dried
³/₄ cup snow peas, chopped
1 bunch green onions (scallions), chopped
2 tbsp arugula

1 Cook the pasta in a large saucepan of lightly salted, boiling water for 10-12 minutes, until just cooked or *al dente*.

2 Meanwhile, place the oil, vinegar, mustard, garlic, herbs, and seasoning in a bowl and whisk together until thoroughly combined. Set aside.

3 Place the bell peppers and tomatoes in a bowl. Tear the spinach leaves into smaller pieces, add to the bowl with the snow peas, green onions (scallions), and arugula, and toss the ingredients together.

4 Drain the pasta thoroughly, whisk the dressing once again, and toss the pasta and dressing together. Toss the pasta and vegetables together and serve warm or cold with fresh crusty bread.

NUTRITIONAL ANALYSIS

(figures are per serving)

Calories = 422
Fat = 16.5g
of which saturates = 2.4g
    monounsaturates = 10.1g
    polyunsaturates = 2.8g

Protein = 12.6g
Carbohydrate = 59.5g
Dietary fiber = 6.7g
Sodium = 0.1g

Percentage of total calories from fat = 35%, of which saturates = 5%
Percentage of total calories from carbohydrate = 53%
of which sugars = 10%
Good source of vitamins A & C

CHAPTER FOUR

RICE & GRAINS

There are many types of rice and grains to choose from, which come in an assortment of shapes and sizes, and all varieties are nutritious. They are high in carbohydrates, provide a good source of energy, and are low in fat. Whole-grain varieties are higher in dietary fiber and contain some B vitamins. Rice also contains some protein.
Rice has excellent absorbent properties, and this makes it and other grains ideal for absorbing the flavors from other foods, so creating a wide range of delicious dishes. Often requiring little or no preparation, rice and grains can be used in many dishes including salads, risottos, stir-fries, dressings, soups, and desserts.

BULGUR WHEAT, MUSHROOM, & GARLIC SALAD

Serve this tasty salad as a side salad with chicken or fish, or as a light meal with fresh crusty bread. Bulgur wheat, also known as burghul or bulghur wheat, is obtainable from Middle Eastern stores. If it is hard to find, use cracked wheat.

Preparation time: 10 minutes, plus soaking time for the bulgur wheat
Cooking time: 10 minutes, plus cooking time for the bulgur wheat (if applicable)
Serves 4 as a light meal or 6 as a side salad

1¹/₂ cups bulgur wheat or cracked wheat
2 tsp olive oil
1 red onion, chopped
2 cloves garlic, crushed
2 cups mushrooms, sliced
4 tomatoes, skinned and chopped
salt and freshly ground black pepper
3 tbsp chopped fresh mixed herbs
fat-free French or Italian dressing

1 Soak and cook (if applicable) the bulgur wheat according to the package instructions.

2 Heat the oil in a saucepan, add the onion and garlic, and cook for 5 minutes, stirring occasionally.

3 Add the mushrooms, cover, and cook for 5 minutes, stirring occasionally.

4 Add the drained, cooked bulgur wheat, tomatoes, seasoning, and herbs, and stir to mix. Sprinkle with some French or

Italian dressing and toss together to mix. Serve warm or cold with crusty French bread.

VARIATIONS
● Use zucchini in place of the mushrooms.
● Use 6 shallots in place of the onion.
● Sprinkle the salad with some finely grated fresh Parmesan cheese just before serving.

FRUIT & NUT
PILAF

A combination of mild spices adds subtle flavor to this delicious pilaf, which is ideal for serving on its own as a light meal, or with some crusty bread and broiled fish or meat for a more substantial meal.

Preparation time: 15 minutes

Cooking time: 30 minutes

Serves 4

2 tsp olive oil
2 cloves garlic, crushed
1 onion, chopped
1 small red chili, seeded and finely chopped
1 tsp ground cumin
1 tsp ground coriander (cilantro)
1 cup brown long-grain rice
1 red bell pepper, seeded and diced
$^1/_2$ cup yellow raisins
$^1/_2$ cup pitted dried apricots, chopped
$2^1/_2$ cups vegetable broth
1 tbsp light soy sauce
1 tbsp dry sherry (optional)
salt and freshly ground black pepper
$^1/_2$ cup unsalted cashew nuts or almonds
fresh herb sprigs, to garnish

1 Heat the oil in a large saucepan. Add the garlic, onion, and chili and cook for 2 minutes, stirring. Add the spices and rice and cook for 1 minute, stirring.

2 Add the bell pepper, yellow raisins, apricots, and broth, and mix well. Cover, bring to the boil, and simmer gently for about 25 minutes, until almost all the liquid has been absorbed and the rice is tender, stirring occasionally.

3 Add the seasoning, soy sauce, sherry, if using, and nuts, and stir to mix. Garnish with fresh herb sprigs.

VARIATIONS
● Use white long-grain rice in place of the brown rice.
● Use 1 cup mushrooms or broccoli in place of the bell pepper.
● Use your own mixture of ground spices such as curry powder, Mexican chili powder, and cardamom.

STUFFED PEPPERS WITH TOMATO & CHILI
SALSA

A tomato and chili salsa complements the flavor of the stuffed peppers perfectly in this light meal. Use different colored peppers to make the dish even more appealing.

Preparation time: 35 minutes

Cooking time: 35-40 minutes

Serves 4 (makes 4 peppers)

NUTRITIONAL ANALYSIS
(figures are per serving)

Calories = 336
Fat = 8.9g
of which saturates = 3.3g
    monounsaturates = 3.1g
    polyunsaturates = 1.7g
Protein = 15.7g
Carbohydrate = 51.4g
Dietary fiber = 6.7g
Sodium = 0.3g

Percentage of total calories from fat = 24%
of which saturates = 9%
Percentage of total calories from carbohydrate = 57%
of which sugars = 19%
Good source of
vitamins A, C, & E

FOR THE SALSA
1 tsp olive oil
4 shallots, finely chopped
1 clove garlic, crushed
1 small red chili, seeded and finely chopped
2 cups tomatoes, skinned, seeded, and finely chopped
6 sun-dried tomatoes, soaked in warm water, drained and finely chopped
1 tsp dried herbs
salt and freshly ground black pepper

FOR THE STUFFED PEPPERS
4 large bell peppers
1 tsp olive oil
1 onion, minced
1 clove garlic, crushed
1 cup cooked brown rice
1 large tomato, skinned and finely chopped
1 cup corn kernels, drained
6 tbsp reduced-fat mature Cheddar cheese, finely grated
1 egg, beaten
2 tbsp minced fresh parsley
1 tbsp minced fresh thyme
salt and freshly ground black pepper

1 To make the salsa, heat the oil in a saucepan, add the shallots, garlic, and chili and cook gently for 10 minutes, stirring occasionally.

2 Add the remaining salsa ingredients, mix well, and cook for 5 minutes, stirring occasionally. Allow to cool. The salsa may be served warm or cold.

3 Make the stuffed peppers. Slice the tops off the peppers, and remove and discard the cores and seeds. Blanch the peppers in boiling water for 4 minutes, then drain thoroughly.

4 Heat the oil in a saucepan. Add the onion and garlic and cook for 5 minutes, stirring occasionally. Add the rice, 1 tbsp water, and the remaining ingredients, and mix well.

5 Fill each pepper with some filling and top with the lids. Place in a shallow ovenproof dish and pour a little water around the bases of the peppers.

6 Cover with foil and bake in a preheated oven at 350° for 35-40 minutes, until the peppers feel tender when pierced with a skewer.

7 Serve the stuffed peppers with the tomato and chili salsa, and some crusty whole-wheat bread for a more substantial meal.

VARIATIONS
● Use frozen peas in place of the corn.
● Use other chopped fresh herbs of your choice such as basil and oregano.

SPICY VEGETABLE
COUSCOUS

A spicy vegetable sauce and freshly steamed couscous make a satisfying dinner. Use packaged couscous, which needs little or no cooking.

Preparation time: 15 minutes, plus soaking time for the couscous

Cooking time: 45 minutes

Serves 4

1½ cups couscous
2 tsp olive oil
1 onion, minced
2 cloves garlic, crushed
1 small red chili, seeded and finely chopped
4 carrots, sliced
2 tsp ground cumin
2 tsp ground coriander (cilantro)
1 tsp ground allspice
4 zucchini, sliced
1½ cups mushrooms, sliced
1 red bell pepper, seeded and sliced
14-ounce can chick-peas (garbanzo beans), rinsed and drained
14-ounce can peeled, chopped tomatoes
1¼ cups vegetable broth
salt and freshly ground black pepper
2 tbsp chopped fresh coriander (cilantro)

1 Soak the couscous according to the package instructions.

2 Meanwhile, heat the oil in a large saucepan over which a steamer, metal colander, or sieve will fit. Add the onion, garlic, chili, and carrots and cook gently for 10 minutes, stirring occasionally.

3 Add the spices and cook for 2 minutes, stirring. Add all the remaining ingredients, except the fresh coriander (cilantro), and mix well.

4 Bring to the boil and reduce the heat to simmer the vegetable mixture. Place the couscous in a steamer, colander, or sieve lined with cheesecloth (if the holes are large enough for the couscous to drop through), and place over the vegetables.

5 Cover with a lid and cook gently for 25-30 minutes, until the vegetables are tender and the couscous is hot, stirring both the vegetable mixture and couscous occasionally.

6 Stir the chopped fresh coriander (cilantro) into the couscous and serve the vegetables on a bed of couscous. Serve with warmed or toasted pita pockets.

The vegetable sauce is suitable for freezing.

VARIATIONS
● Serve the cooked vegetables on a bed of cooked cracked wheat or brown rice, in place of the couscous.
● Use 2 cups fresh tomatoes (skinned, seeded, and finely chopped) in place of the canned tomatoes.
● Use your own choice of ground spices such as chili powder, cinnamon, and allspice.

NUTRITIONAL ANALYSIS
(figures are per serving)

Calories = 384
Fat = 6.2g
of which saturates = 0.7g
    monounsaturates = 1.9g
    polyunsaturates = 1.8g
Protein = 15.4g
Carbohydrate = 71.9g
Dietary fiber = 7.5g
Sodium = 0.4g

Percentage of total calories from fat = 15%
of which saturates = 2%
Percentage of total calories from carbohydrate = 70%
of which sugars = 13%
Good source of vitamins A & C

1 Heat the oil in a large saucepan, add the onion, garlic, and bell pepper and cook for 3 minutes, stirring.

2 Add the rice and mushrooms and cook for 1 minute, stirring. Add the broth, wine, and seasoning and mix well.

3 Bring to the boil and simmer, uncovered, for 25-30 minutes, until almost all the liquid has been absorbed, stirring occasionally.

4 Stir in the chicken, peas, lima beans, chick-peas (garbanzo beans), and yellow raisins, and cook gently for about 10 minutes, stirring occasionally.

5 Stir in the chopped herbs and serve the risotto immediately with fresh crusty bread and a mixed leaf side salad.

6 Garnish the risotto with Parmesan shavings just before serving, if liked.

VARIATIONS

● Use cooked, unsmoked chicken in place of the smoked chicken.
● Use frozen green beans in place of the peas.
● Use corn in place of the lima beans.

SMOKED CHICKEN & MUSHROOM
RISOTTO

Serve this tempting risotto for a substantial lunch, or dinner.

Preparation time: 10 minutes

Cooking time: 45 minutes

Serves 4

2 tsp olive oil
1 onion, chopped
2 cloves garlic, crushed
1 red bell pepper, seeded and diced
1 cup long-grain brown rice
1 cup mushrooms, sliced
2¹/₂ cups chicken or vegetable broth
1¹/₄ cups dry white wine
salt and freshly ground black pepper
1 cup diced cooked skinless, boneless smoked chicken
¹/₂ cup frozen peas
¹/₂ cup frozen lima beans
¹/₂ cup canned and drained chick-peas (garbanzo beans)
3 tbsp yellow raisins
2 tbsp chopped fresh mixed herbs
Parmesan shavings, to garnish (optional)

NUTRITIONAL ANALYSIS

(figures are per serving)

Calories = 519	Protein = 25.8g
Fat = 6.8g	Carbohydrate = 81.6g
of which saturates = 1.4g	Dietary fiber = 7.8g
monounsaturates = 2.5g	Sodium = 0.4g
polyunsaturates = 1.9g	

Percentage of total calories from fat = 12%
of which saturates = 2%
Percentage of total calories from carbohydrate = 59%
of which sugars = 16%

TUNA & SHRIMP
RISOTTO

This tuna and shrimp risotto is quite similar to a paella. Serve on its own or with crusty bread and a side salad as an entrée.

Preparation time: 10 minutes

Cooking time: 45 minutes

Serves 4

1¹/₄ cups long-grain brown rice
1 onion, chopped
1 clove garlic, crushed
1¹/₄ cups mushrooms, sliced
2¹/₂ cups fish or vegetable broth
2 cups dry white wine
pinch of ground saffron
salt and freshly ground black pepper
7-ounce can tuna in water,
drained and flaked
8 cooked, peeled, and deveined jumbo shrimp
7-ounce can corn kernels, drained
³/₄ cup frozen peas
2 tbsp minced fresh parsley
2 tbsp finely grated fresh Parmesan cheese
whole cooked jumbo shrimp and fresh herb sprigs,
to garnish

1 Place the rice, onion, garlic, mushrooms, broth, wine, saffron, and seasoning in a saucepan and mix well.

2 Bring to the boil and simmer, uncovered, for 30-35 minutes, or until the rice is tender, stirring occasionally.

3 Add the tuna, shrimp, corn, and peas, and mix well. Cook over a higher heat for 5 minutes, stirring frequently, until most of the liquid has been absorbed. Add the parsley and stir to mix.

4 Serve immediately, sprinkled with Parmesan cheese and garnished with whole jumbo shrimp and fresh herb sprigs. Serve with warm, freshly-baked bread and a sweet pepper and tomato side salad.

NUTRITIONAL ANALYSIS

(figures are per serving)

Calories = 545
Fat = 5.9g
of which saturates = 2.0g
     monounsaturates = 1.3g
     polyunsaturates = 1.6g

Protein = 36.1g
Carbohydrate = 73.5g
Dietary fiber = 5.1g
Sodium = 1.5g

Percentage of total calories from fat = 10%
of which saturates = 3%
Percentage of total calories from carbohydrate = 51%, of which sugars = 6%

PLUM & LEMON
RICE DESSERT

A layer of juicy plums is topped with creamy rice flavored with a hint of lemon in this delicious dessert, which can be enjoyed hot or cold.

Preparation time: 10 minutes
Cooking time: 1 hour, 45 minutes
Serves 4

1/4 cup short-grain, white rice
1 1/4 cups low-fat or 2% milk
finely grated rind of 1 lemon
1 tbsp soft margarine
3 tbsp sugar
4 ripe plums, pitted and sliced
1/2 tsp ground cinnamon
lemon rind strips, to decorate

1 Place the rice, milk, lemon rind, and margarine in a heavy-based saucepan. Heat gently, stirring continuously, until the mixture comes to the boil.

2 Reduce the heat and simmer gently for 45-60 minutes, until the mixture has thickened and the rice grains are tender, stirring frequently. Remove from the heat and stir in the sugar.

3 Combine the plum slices and cinnamon, and arrange the plums in the base of a lightly greased ovenproof dish. Pour the rice mixture over the plums and level the surface.

4 Bake in a preheated oven at 325° for 35-45 minutes, until lightly browned on top.

5 Decorate with pared lemon rind strips and serve hot or cold with low-fat ice cream or reduced-fat cream.

VARIATIONS
● Use other fruits such as apricots, peaches, or nectarines in place of the plums.
● Use ground mixed spice or ground ginger in place of the cinnamon.
● Use the finely grated rind of 1 lime or 1 small orange in place of the lemon rind.
● Make individual desserts in small ramekin dishes and bake for about 30 minutes.

NUTRITIONAL ANALYSIS

(figures are per serving)

Calories = 209
Fat = 6.1g
of which saturates = 2.3g
    monounsaturates = 1.6g
    polyunsaturates = 1.7g

Protein = 6.4g
Carbohydrate = 34.4g
Dietary fiber = 0.8g
Sodium = 0.1g

Percentage of total calories from fat = 26%, of which saturates = 10%
Percentage of total calories from carbohydrate = 62%
of which sugars = 41%

FRESH ORANGE
FARINA DESSERT

This is a quick and easy farina (cream of wheat) dessert to make, with the subtle flavor of orange.

Preparation time: 15 minutes

Cooking time: 30 minutes

Serves 4

2¹/₂ cups low-fat or 2% milk
1 tbsp soft margarine
finely grated rind of 1 orange
¹/₄ cup farina (cream of wheat)
2 tbsp sugar
freshly grated nutmeg
pared orange rind, to decorate

1 Place the milk, margarine, and orange rind in a saucepan and bring gently to the boil.

2 Sprinkle the semolina over the milk, stirring quickly. Return to the boil, stirring, then cook gently for 2 minutes, stirring.

3 Stir in the sugar, then pour the mixture into a lightly greased ovenproof dish. Sprinkle some grated nutmeg over the top.

4 Bake in a preheated oven at 400° for about 30 minutes, until lightly browned on top.

5 Decorate with pared orange rind and serve hot with fresh fruits such as sliced peaches, pears, or raspberries.

VARIATIONS
● Use the finely grated rind of 1 lemon or 1 lime in place of the orange rind.
● For a chocolate and orange farina dessert, break 2 squares (2 ounces) semi-sweet baking chocolate into pieces and melt. Combine with the milk. Alternatively, omit the orange rind and just use the semi-sweet chocolate.
● Use whole-wheat farina in place of white farina.

NUTRITIONAL ANALYSIS
(figures are per serving)

Calories = 201
Fat = 5.8g
of which saturates = 2.2g
      monounsaturates = 1.6g
      polyunsaturates = 1.7g
Protein = 6.6g
Carbohydrate = 32.9g
Dietary fiber = 0.3g
Sodium = 0.1g

Percentage of total calories from fat = 26%
of which saturates = 10%
Percentage of total calories from
carbohydrate = 61%, of which sugars = 41%

CHAPTER FIVE

POTATOES

*P*otatoes are low in fat, contain some vitamin C, and are high in carbohydrates, making
them a good source of energy. They are also a good source of fiber, especially when baked
in their skins. The potato comes in many varieties, and is a versatile vegetable that can be
cooked and eaten in many different ways. Often served as an accompanying vegetable,
potatoes are also ideal for a wide variety of dishes such as vegetable bakes, baked potatoes
with toppings, salads, casseroles, stews, pasties, turnovers, and soups.
Fat is often added to potatoes. For example, they are roasted in oil, creamed, or served as
french fries. All of these cooking methods can increase the fat content of the potatoes
considerably. Fortunately, there are healthy ways to enjoy your favorite kinds of potato.
Delicious roasted potatoes can be made by using the minimum amount of shortening or by
dry-roasting them. Instead of deep-frying french fries, try
oven-baked fries which are lower in fat.

POTATO & CARROT
SOUP

*A tempting, flavorful soup,
this dish is ideal as an appetizer
for cold winter nights
or as a takeout lunchtime warmer.*

Preparation time: 10 minutes

Cooking time: 30 minutes

Serves 4

*1 onion, minced
1 pound potatoes, washed and cut into chunks
8 ounces carrots, sliced
3 sticks celery, sliced
3³/₄ cups vegetable broth
1 bay leaf
salt and freshly ground black pepper
2 tbsp minced fresh parsley*

1 Place all the ingredients, except the parsley, in a large saucepan and mix well.

2 Cover, bring to the boil, and simmer for 20-25 minutes, until the vegetables are tender, stirring occasionally.

3 Remove from the heat and set aside to cool slightly. Remove and discard the bay leaf, then place the mixture in a blender or food processor and blend until smooth.

4 Return to the saucepan and add the parsley. Adjust the seasoning and reheat gently. Serve with some fresh crusty French bread or garlic bread croutons.

VARIATIONS
● Use ³/₄ cup sliced leeks (trimmed weight) in place of the onion.
● Use rutabaga or parsnips in place of the carrots.
● Use chopped fresh mixed herbs in place of the parsley.
● Use a bouquet garni in place of the bay leaf.

MOROCCAN POTATO
SALAD

This delicately spiced potato salad is delicious served as an appetizer or as an accompaniment to broiled fish or meat. Alternatively, serve it as a picnic treat.

Preparation time: 20 minutes

Cooking time: 20 minutes

Serves 6 as an appetizer or side salad

2 pounds small new potatoes, washed
3 tbsp tomato juice
1/2 tsp ground cumin
1/2 tsp ground paprika
1/2 tsp ground coriander (cilantro)
2 1/2 tsp ground turmeric
1/2 tsp ground cinnamon
1/2 tsp ground ginger
1 clove garlic, crushed (optional)
2 bunches green onions (scallions), chopped
1 yellow bell pepper, seeded and diced
2-3 tbsp chopped fresh coriander (cilantro)
5 tbsp reduced-calorie mayonnaise
5 tbsp low-fat plain yogurt
salt and freshly ground black pepper

1 Cook the potatoes in a large saucepan of lightly salted, boiling water for 10-15 minutes, until cooked and tender. Drain thoroughly and allow to cool completely.

2 Place the tomato juice, spices, and garlic, if using, in a small saucepan and cook gently for 2 minutes, stirring. Allow to cool slightly.

3 Place the cold potatoes in a large bowl, add the green onions (scallions), yellow bell pepper, and coriander (cilantro), and stir to mix.

4 Place the mayonnaise, yogurt, spice mixture, and seasoning in a small bowl and mix together thoroughly. Pour the dressing over the potatoes and toss together to mix.

5 Cover and set aside for 30 minutes before serving. Alternatively, cover and chill in the refrigerator until ready to use.

6 As a side salad, serve with broiled fish such as sole or monkfish, or with lean meat such as chicken or lamb.

VARIATIONS

● Use 1 large minced red onion in place of the green onions (scallions).
● Use old potatoes, peeled and cut into small chunks, in place of the new potatoes.
● This salad may be served warm. Toss the warm cooked potatoes with the dressing and serve.

HERBED CHICKEN
& POTATO BAKE

Preparation time: 35 minutes

Cooking time: 1 hour

Serves 6 as an entrée

1 pound potatoes, washed and cut into thin slices
1 tbsp olive oil
3 tbsp low-fat spread
3 tbsp all-purpose flour
2¹/₂ cups chicken or vegetable broth, cooled
1¹/₄ cups low-fat or 2% milk
1 pound shallots
1¹/₄ cups mushrooms, sliced
1 cup diced cooked skinless, boneless chicken
1 cup frozen or canned corn kernels
14-ounce can black-eyed peas, rinsed and drained
2 tbsp minced fresh coriander (cilantro)
salt and freshly ground black pepper
fresh coriander (cilantro) leaves, to garnish

1 Parboil the potatoes in a saucepan of boiling water for 4 minutes, then drain thoroughly, and toss the potato slices in the oil. Set aside.

2 Place the low-fat spread, flour, broth, and milk in a saucepan. Heat gently, whisking continuously, until the sauce comes to the boil and thickens. Simmer gently for 3 minutes, stirring.

3 Peel the shallots, slice them thinly, and add to the sauce with the mushrooms, chicken, corn, black-eyed peas, coriander (cilantro), and seasoning, mixing well. Place the mixture in a shallow ovenproof casserole dish.

4 Arrange the potato slices over the chicken mixture, covering it completely.

5 Cover with foil and bake in a preheated oven at 400° for about 1 hour, until the potatoes are cooked, tender, and browned on top. Remove the foil for the final 20 minutes.

6 Garnish with fresh coriander leaves and serve with steamed vegetables and crusty bread.

VARIATIONS
● Use cooked turkey or lean ham in place of the chicken.
● Use 1 diced red or yellow bell pepper in place of the mushrooms.

NUTRITIONAL ANALYSIS

(figures are per serving)

Calories = 319
Fat = 8.2g
of which saturates = 2.0g
monounsaturates = 2.3g
polyunsaturates = 1.9g
Protein = 21.8g
Carbohydrate = 42.3g
Dietary fiber = 6.0g
Sodium = 0.5g

Percentage of total calories from fat = 23%
of which saturates = 6%
Percentage of total calories from carbohydrate = 50%
of which sugars = 13%

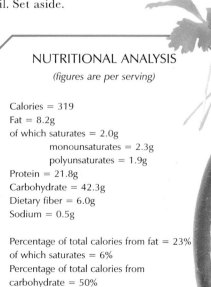

POTATO, CARROT, & PARSNIP
BAKE

*Root vegetables such as potatoes, carrots, and parsnips
are a tasty trio when cooked together in this simple but flavorful dish.
Serve with oven-baked fish or chicken and fresh vegetables.*

Preparation time: 35 minutes

Cooking time: 30 minutes

Serves 4 as an accompanying vegetable dish

4 medium potatoes, peeled and diced
2 carrots, thinly sliced
2 parsnips, peeled and sliced
½ cup finely grated reduced-fat mature Cheddar
cheese
2 tbsp chopped fresh chives
salt and freshly ground black pepper
fresh herb sprigs, to garnish

1 Cook the vegetables in a large saucepan of lightly salted, boiling water for about 20 minutes, until tender.

2 Drain and mash thoroughly. Add the cheese, chives, and seasoning and mix well.

3 Place the mixture in a lightly greased ovenproof dish and level the surface.

4 Bake in a preheated oven at 350° for about 30 minutes, until the top is lightly browned.

5 Garnish with fresh herb sprigs. Serve with oven-baked fish, such as trout or salmon, and steamed fresh seasonal vegetables, such as snow-peas and baby corn.

NUTRITIONAL ANALYSIS

(figures are per serving)

Calories = 196
Fat = 4.2g
of which saturates = 2.2g
monounsaturates = 1.2g
polyunsaturates = 0.4g
Protein = 10.4g
Carbohydrate = 30.8g
Dietary fiber = 5.4g
Sodium = 0.2g

Percentage of total calories from fat = 19%
of which saturates = 10%
Percentage of total calories from
carbohydrate = 59%, of which sugars = 15%
Good source of vitamin A

VARIATIONS

● Use rutabaga or jicama in place of the parsnips.

● Use other reduced-fat hard cheese such as Monterey jack in place of the Cheddar cheese.

● Use sweet potatoes or a mixture of sweet and white potatoes.

● Reserve a little of the cheese and sprinkle it over the bake before cooking.

55

BAKED POTATO
TOPPINGS

Baked potatoes are always a popular choice, especially when topped with flavorful savory mixtures such as these. Serve the baked potatoes with a topping of your choice and enjoy a nutritious light meal. Each topping is enough for 4 large baked potatoes.

Preparation time: 5 minutes, plus preparing the filling
Cooking time: 1-1½ hours
Serves 4 (makes 4 potatoes)

4 large baking potatoes, washed and dried

Pierce the potatoes with a fork. Bake near the top of a preheated oven at 400° for 1-1½ hours, until tender throughout. Cut a cross in the top of the potato or cut the potato in half to serve, and top with one of the following tasty toppings.

SMOKED BACON, EGG, & CORN
4 slices lean smoked bacon
4 medium eggs, hard-boiled and cooled
7-ounce can corn kernels, drained
4 tbsp reduced-calorie mayonnaise
2 tbsp minced chives
salt and freshly ground black pepper

Broil the bacon slices for 3-5 minutes, turning once, until cooked and crispy. Meanwhile, peel the eggs. Mash or finely chop the eggs and mix with the corn, mayonnaise, chives, and seasoning. Dice the cooked bacon. Cut open the baked potatoes and spoon the egg mixture over them. Sprinkle with the bacon and serve with a mixed tomato, bell pepper, and onion salad.

PINK SALMON & SOUR CREAM
7-ounce can salmon in water, drained and flaked
2 bunches green onions (scallions), chopped
1 beefsteak tomato, chopped
²/₃ cup sour cream
salt and freshly ground black pepper

Mix together the salmon, green onions (scallions), tomato, sour cream, and seasoning. Cut open the baked potatoes and spoon the salmon mixture over them. Serve with a mixed green side salad.

SPICY TOMATO & MUSHROOM
1 pound tomatoes, skinned and chopped
1 small onion, minced
1 cup mushrooms, finely chopped
1 clove garlic, crushed
1 tsp chili powder
1 tsp ground cumin
salt and freshly ground black pepper

Place all the ingredients in a saucepan and mix well. Cover, bring to the boil, and simmer gently for 10 minutes, stirring occasionally. Remove the lid and cook for a further 5 minutes, until the vegetables are tender, stirring occasionally. Cut open the baked potatoes and spoon the tomato sauce over them. Serve with a mixed green side salad.

NUTRITIONAL ANALYSIS

(figures are per serving of Smoked Bacon, Egg, & Corn Baked Potatoes)

Calories = 515	Protein = 22.1g
Fat = 13.2g	Carbohydrate = 82.2g
of which saturates = 2.5g	Dietary fiber = 6.5g
monounsaturates = 3.6g	Sodium = 0.8g
polyunsaturates = 1.3g	

Percentage of total calories from fat = 23%, of which saturates = 4%
Percentage of total calories from carbohydrate = 60%
of which sugars = 5%
Good source of vitamin C

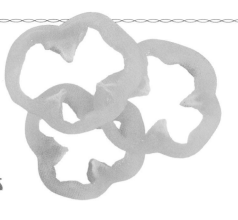

HERBED POTATO
CAKES

*A delicious accompaniment to broiled lean meat or fish,
these herbed potato cakes are simple to prepare and cook. The mixture
can also be made in advance and refrigerated until required.*

Preparation time: 30 minutes, plus cooling time
Cooking time: 10-15 minutes

Makes 8 potato cakes

*8 medium potatoes
2 tbsp vegetable broth
4 leeks, trimmed and finely chopped
1 clove garlic, crushed
4 tbsp finely grated reduced-fat mature
Cheddar cheese
1 egg, beaten
1 tbsp chopped fresh parsley
1 tbsp chopped fresh chives
salt and freshly ground black pepper
1 tsp olive oil*

1 Cook the potatoes in a saucepan of lightly salted, boiling water for about 20 minutes, until cooked and tender. Drain and mash thoroughly.

2 Meanwhile, place the broth, leeks, and garlic in a saucepan, cover and cook gently for 10-15 minutes until tender, stirring occasionally. Drain thoroughly.

3 Add the mashed potatoes, cheese, egg, herbs, and seasoning and mix well. Set aside to cool completely.

4 On a lightly floured surface, divide the mixture into 8 portions and shape each portion into a patty, and flatten slightly.

5 Heat the oil in a large nonstick skillet. Fry the potato cakes until golden brown on both sides, turning once.

6 Serve with broiled lean meat such as chicken, steak, lamb, or pork and seasonal fresh vegetables such as baby carrots and green beans.

VARIATIONS
● Use sweet potatoes or a mixture of sweet and white potatoes.
● Use 1 minced onion in place of the leeks.
● Use other reduced-fat hard cheese such as Monterey jack.

NUTRITIONAL ANALYSIS
(figures are per potato cake)

Calories = 90
Fat = 2.4g
of which   saturates = 0.9g
   monounsaturates = 0.9g
   polyunsaturates = 0.3g

Protein = 5.0g
Carbohydrate = 12.6g
Dietary fiber = 1.5g
Sodium = 0.06g

Percentage of total calories from fat = 25%, of which saturates = 9%
Percentage of total calories from carbohydrate = 53%
of which sugars = 4%

LAMB
& VEGETABLE
CURRY

Preparation time: 25 minutes

Cooking time: 1 hour

Serves 4

2 tsp sunflower oil
12 ounces lean lamb fillet, cut into small dice
1 onion, sliced
2 cloves garlic, crushed
1 small red chili, seeded and finely chopped
1-inch piece fresh root ginger, peeled and minced
1 tbsp ground coriander (cilantro)
2 tsp ground cumin
1 tsp ground cinnamon
1 tsp ground turmeric
pinch of ground cloves (optional)
14-ounce can peeled, chopped tomatoes
1¹/₄ cups vegetable broth
1 pound small new potatoes, washed and dried
1 medium rutabaga, diced
2 leeks, trimmed and sliced
1 cup sliced mushrooms
2 medium carrots, sliced
salt and freshly ground black pepper
¹/₂ cup yellow raisins
2 tbsp chopped fresh coriander (cilantro)
fresh coriander (cilantro) sprigs, to garnish

1 Heat the oil in a large nonstick saucepan. Add the lamb and cook for 5 minutes, stirring occasionally. Remove from the pan using a slotted spoon and keep warm.

2 Add the onion, garlic, chili, and ginger to the pan and cook gently for 3 minutes, stirring. Add the spices and cook for 1 minute, stirring.

3 Add the lamb and all the remaining ingredients, except the yellow raisins and fresh coriander (cilantro), and mix well.

4 Cover, bring to the boil, and simmer for 45-60 minutes, until the lamb is cooked and tender, stirring occasionally. Add the

yellow raisins 10 minutes before the end of the cooking time.

5 Add the chopped fresh coriander (cilantro) and stir to mix. Garnish with fresh coriander (cilantro) sprigs and serve with warm crusty bread or pita pockets, or on a bed of boiled rice.

VARIATIONS
● Use lean beef or chicken in place of the lamb.
● Use parsnips, turnips, or jicama in place of the rutabaga.
● Use 2 cups skinned and chopped fresh tomatoes in place of the canned tomatoes.

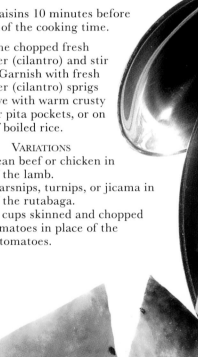

BRAISED BEEF
& MUSHROOMS WITH NEW POTATOES & BASIL

Preparation time: 20 minutes

Cooking time: 2 ½ hours

Serves 4

12 ounces lean stewing or braising steak, diced
2 tbsp all-purpose flour, seasoned
2 tsp sunflower oil
4 cups pearl onions, peeled
1 clove garlic, crushed
2 carrots, sliced
1¼ cups button mushrooms
2 sticks celery, chopped
1¼ cups beef broth
⅔ cup red wine
1 tbsp tomato paste
salt and freshly ground black pepper
1 bouquet garni (thyme, bay leaf, and parsley tied in a bunch)
1 cup frozen lima beans
3 cups small new potatoes, washed
1 tbsp minced fresh basil
1 tbsp minced fresh parsley

1 Toss the beef in the seasoned flour. Heat the oil in a large nonstick saucepan, add the onions and garlic, and cook gently for 5 minutes, stirring occasionally.

2 Add the beef and flour, and cook gently for 5 minutes, stirring occasionally. Add the carrots, mushrooms, celery, broth, wine, tomato paste, seasoning, and bouquet garni, and mix well.

3 Bring to the boil, stirring, then cover and simmer gently for 2 hours, stirring occasionally.

4 Add the lima beans, bring back to the boil, and simmer gently for a further 30 minutes, until the beef is tender. Remove the bouquet garni.

5 Meanwhile, cook the potatoes in a saucepan of lightly salted, boiling water for 10-15 minutes, until cooked and tender. Drain thoroughly and toss with the fresh herbs.

6 Serve the braised beef with the boiled new potatoes and steamed seasonal fresh vegetables such as green beans and shredded cabbage.

VARIATION

● Use lean lamb in place of the beef.

NUTRITIONAL ANALYSIS

(figures are per serving)

Calories = 423
Fat = 7.7g
of which saturates = 2.5g
monounsaturates = 3.1g
polyunsaturates = 1.2g
Protein = 31.0g
Carbohydrate = 54.9g
Dietary fiber = 9.4g
Sodium = 0.2g

Percentage of total calories from fat = 16%
of which saturates = 5%
Percentage of total calories from carbohydrate = 49%
of which sugars = 13%

CHAPTER SIX

BEANS & LENTILS

*B*eans and lentils are the edible seeds of pod-bearing plants of the legume family, and
are available in many varieties. Some, such as lima beans and peas, are eaten fresh,
but many, such as chick-peas (garbanzo beans) and kidney beans, are used in dried
or canned forms. Frozen beans are also widely available while other beans are fermented
or processed to produce products such as flour, oil, or fresh and dried bean curd. Beans
and lentils are naturally low in fat and high in carbohydrates, protein, and fiber,
and contain a variety of essential vitamins and minerals.
Because generally they do not have a strong taste of their own, beans and lentils are ideal
for mixing with more strongly flavored, richer foods. Once they have been cooked, they
keep well in the refrigerator and also reheat well. Canned beans and lentils are ready
to eat, so they may be added to cooked dishes such as chili con carne,
or served cold in dishes such as salads.

CORN & PEA
SOUP

*This nutritious soup makes an excellent appetizer
for a meal or a quick snack.*

Preparation time: 20 minutes
Cooking time: 30 minutes

Serves 4

2 tsp sunflower oil
1 onion, minced
2 sticks celery, finely chopped
1 pound shelled fresh or frozen peas
1 bunch watercress, washed and chopped
3 cups vegetable broth
$^1/_2$ tsp sugar
salt and freshly ground black pepper
1 cup canned corn kernels

1 Heat the oil in a large saucepan. Add
the onion and celery, and cook gently for
5 minutes, stirring occasionally.

2 Add the peas, watercress, broth, sugar,
and seasoning and mix well. Cover, bring
to the boil, and simmer gently for 25-30
minutes, until the vegetables are tender,
stirring occasionally.

3 Remove the pan from the heat
and allow to cool slightly. Place
the mixture in a blender or food
processor and blend until smooth.

4 Return the mixture to the
saucepan and add the corn. Reheat
the soup until piping hot, stirring,
then serve with some warm, freshly
baked bread.

VARIATIONS
● Use lima beans in place
of the peas.
● Use 1 red onion or 4 leeks,
trimmed and finely chopped, in
place of the onion.
● Use half milk and
half broth.

ROASTED PEPPER
& BROWN LENTIL DIP

*This delicious dip can also be served as a pâté
with fresh crusty bread or toast.*

Preparation time: 30 minutes
Cooking time: 10 minutes
Serves 6

1 cup brown lentils
vegetable broth
1 bay leaf
2 large mild sweet red peppers (such as chipotle)
1 onion, minced
1 clove garlic, crushed
³/₄ cup mushrooms, minced
6 tbsp reduced-fat mature Cheddar cheese, finely grated
2 tbsp chopped fresh coriander (cilantro)
salt and freshly ground black pepper
2 tbsp low-fat plain yogurt (optional)
fresh herb sprigs, to garnish

1 Place the lentils in a saucepan and cover with plenty of vegetable broth. Add the bay leaf and stir to mix. Cover, bring to the boil, then simmer gently for 30–40 minutes, until the lentils are tender, stirring occasionally. Drain thoroughly and discard the bay leaf.

2 Meanwhile, broil the peppers until they are charred and blistered all over.

3 Remove from the heat, cover with a clean, damp cloth, allow to cool slightly, then peel off the skins. Core, seed, and dice the flesh.

4 Put the onion, garlic, mushrooms, and peppers in a saucepan with 2 tbsp broth. Cover and cook gently for 10 minutes, until the vegetables are tender, stirring occasionally.

5 Add the cooked lentils, cheese, coriander (cilantro), and seasoning, and mix well. Place the mixture in a blender or food processor and blend until smooth.

6 Transfer to a serving dish and allow to cool. Once cool, stir in the yogurt, if using. Cover and chill in the refrigerator before serving.

7 Garnish with herbs and serve with sliced vegetables and breadsticks (grissini).

SWEET-&-SOUR
MIXED-BEAN SALAD

Preparation time: 20 minutes
Cooking time: 10 minutes
Serves 4

1³/₄ cups green beans, trimmed and halved
1 small red onion, sliced
1 small red bell pepper, seeded and diced
1 small yellow bell pepper, seeded and diced
¹/₂ cup raisins
7-ounce can corn kernels, drained
14-ounce can red kidney beans, rinsed and drained
14-ounce can chick-peas (garbanzo beans), rinsed and drained
2-3 tbsp minced fresh parsley

FOR THE DRESSING
3 tbsp olive oil
3 tbsp unsweetened apple juice
2 tbsp red wine vinegar
2 tbsp clear honey
2 tbsp light soy sauce
2 tbsp tomato ketchup
2 tbsp medium sherry
1 clove garlic, crushed
1 tsp ground ginger
salt and freshly ground black pepper

1 Steam the green beans over a pan of simmering water for about 10 minutes, until just tender. Drain and rinse under cold water to cool them. Drain well.

2 Place the cooled green beans, onion, bell peppers, raisins, corn, kidney beans, chick-peas (garbanzo beans), and parsley in a large bowl and mix together.

3 Place all the dressing ingredients in a small bowl and whisk together until thoroughly mixed. Pour over the mixed beans and toss together to mix.

4 Serve the mixed-bean salad with crusty French bread or toasted pita pockets.

VARIATIONS
● Use your own selection of canned beans.
● Use chopped fresh mixed herbs in place of the parsley.

● When making the dressing, place all the ingredients in a clean screw-top jar. Screw the top on the jar and shake well until the ingredients are thoroughly mixed.

RED BEAN

& THREE-MUSHROOM SALAD

A colorful combination of beans and mushrooms tossed together in a light dressing, this recipe is ideal as an entrée salad served with warm bread or as a nutritious packed lunch.

Preparation time: 20 minutes
Serves 4 as an entrée

two 14-ounce cans red kidney beans,
rinsed and drained
2 bunches green onions (scallions), chopped
1 bunch radishes, sliced
¹/₂ cup yellow raisins
³/₄ cup brown cap or chestnut mushrooms, sliced
³/₄ cup button mushrooms, halved
1 cup oyster mushrooms
3 tbsp olive oil
3 tbsp cider vinegar
1 tbsp whole-grain mustard
1 clove garlic, crushed
1 tbsp minced fresh parsley
1 tbsp minced chives
salt and freshly ground black pepper

1 Place the kidney beans, green onions (scallions), radishes, yellow raisins, and mushrooms in a bowl and stir to mix.

2 Place the oil, vinegar, mustard, garlic, herbs, and seasoning in a small bowl and whisk together until thoroughly mixed.

3 Drizzle the dressing over the bean and mushroom salad, and toss together to mix. Serve with warm freshly baked bread.

VARIATIONS
● Use raisins or chopped, pitted dried apricots in place of the yellow raisins.
● Use 1 minced red onion in place of the green onions (scallions).

SMOKED TOFU & VEGETABLE
KABOBS

Serve these kabobs for lunch or dinner on a bed
of cooked cracked wheat, couscous, or boiled rice. Alternatively,
serve with a mixed leaf salad and some fresh crusty bread.

Preparation time: 25 minutes

Cooking time: 10-15 minutes

Makes 8 kabobs

FOR THE TOMATO SAUCE
1 cup canned peeled, chopped tomatoes
²/₃ cup tomato juice
1 tbsp tomato paste
1 clove garlic, crushed
2 shallots, minced
salt and freshly ground black pepper
1 tbsp chopped fresh basil

FOR THE KABOBS
³/₄ cup smoked tofu, cut into 8 cubes
1 red bell pepper, seeded and cut into 8 pieces
1 small yellow bell pepper, seeded
and cut into 8 pieces
2 small zucchini, each cut into 6 slices
8 cherry tomatoes
8 button mushrooms
8 pearl or button onions, peeled
8 boiled small potatoes
1 tbsp olive oil
1 tbsp lemon juice
1 tsp dried mixed herbs
salt and freshly ground black pepper
fresh basil sprigs, to garnish

1 To make the tomato sauce, place all the ingredients, except the basil, in a saucepan and stir to mix. Bring to the boil and simmer gently, uncovered, for about 15 minutes, stirring occasionally. Add the basil and mix well. This sauce may be served hot or cold and it can be puréed in a liquidizer before serving, if preferred.

2 To make the kabobs, thread the tofu and vegetables onto 8 skewers, dividing the ingredients equally.

3 Mix together the oil, lemon juice, herbs, and seasoning, and brush the mixture over the kabobs.

4 Broil the kabobs over a barbecue or under a preheated broiler for about 10-15 minutes, until the tofu and vegetables are cooked to your liking, turning frequently. Brush the kabobs with any remaining oil mixture while they are cooking, to prevent them from drying out.

5 Garnish with fresh basil sprigs and serve with the tomato sauce.

VARIATIONS
● Use other flavored tofu such as original or marinated in place of the smoked tofu.
● Use your own selection of vegetables and use cubes of lean meat such as chicken or beef in place of the tofu.

NUTRITIONAL ANALYSIS
(figures are per serving)

Calories = 165
Fat = 5.5g
of which saturates = 0.8g
    monounsaturates = 2.4g
    polyunsaturates = 1.5g

Protein = 8.0g
Carbohydrate = 22.3g
Dietary fiber = 4.3g
Sodium = 0.01g

Percentage of total calories from fat = 30%, of which saturates = 4%
Percentage of total calories from carbohydrate = 51%, of which sugars = 27%
Good source of vitamin C

BEEF & BEAN
BURGERS

The delicious combination of ground beef, beans, and spices ensures that these extra-large burgers are a popular choice for brunch, lunch, or dinner.

Preparation time: 25 minutes

Cooking time: 10-15 minutes

Serves 4 (makes 4 large burgers)

9 ounces extra-lean ground beef
1 onion, minced
1 clove garlic, crushed
14-ounce can red kidney beans, rinsed, drained, and mashed
4 tbsp wheatgerm
2 small carrots, coarsely shredded
1 egg, beaten
1 tsp ground cumin
1 tsp ground coriander (cilantro)
1 tsp chili powder
3 tbsp minced parsley
salt and freshly ground black pepper
1 tbsp sunflower oil
4 large whole-wheat or white hamburger rolls,
tomato slices and shredded lettuce, to serve

1 Place the ground beef, onion, garlic, kidney beans, wheatgerm, carrots, egg, spices, parsley, and seasoning in a bowl and mix thoroughly. On a lightly floured surface, shape the mixture into 4 large round patties and flatten them slightly.

2 Heat the oil in a good quality nonstick skillet and cook the burgers for about 10-15 minutes, turning once, until browned on the outside and cooked to your liking.

3 Serve each burger in a hamburger roll and top with tomato slices and shredded lettuce. Serve with homemade low-calorie coleslaw.

These burgers are suitable for freezing before they have been cooked.

VARIATIONS
● The hamburgers can be brushed lightly with oil and broiled instead of fried.
● Use the mixture to make 6 or 8 smaller burgers, if you prefer.
● Use other lean ground meats such as pork, lamb, or turkey in place of the beef.
● Use 2 small leeks (trimmed weight), minced, in place of the onion.
● Use other canned beans such as black-eyed peas or chick-peas (garbanzo beans) in place of the kidney beans.

NUTRITIONAL ANALYSIS
(figures are per burger including roll & salad)

Calories = 543
Fat = 14.3g
of which saturates = 4.2g
    monounsaturates = 5.8g
    polyunsaturates = 2.2g

Protein = 33.2g
Carbohydrate = 75.6g
Dietary fiber = 9.2g
Sodium = 0.8g

Percentage of total calories from fat = 24%, of which saturates = 7%
Percentage of total calories from carbohydrate = 52%, of which sugars = 8%
Good source of B vitamins & vitamin E

VEGETARIAN CHILI

An appetizing and colorful meat-free dish, which is ideal served on its own or with boiled rice for lunch or a main meal.

Preparation time: 20 minutes

Cooking time: 50 minutes

Serves 4

1 tsp olive oil
1 onion, sliced
2 cloves garlic, crushed
3 leeks, sliced
1 tbsp all-purpose flour
1¼ cups vegetable broth
4 sticks celery, chopped
1 red bell pepper, seeded and diced
1 yellow bell pepper, seeded and diced
1 cup thinly sliced carrots
14-ounce can peeled, chopped tomatoes
2 tbsp tomato paste
1 tsp hot chili powder
1 tsp ground cumin
½ tsp sugar
salt and freshly ground black pepper
14-ounce can red kidney beans, rinsed and drained
14-ounce can chick-peas (garbanzo beans), rinsed and drained
minced fresh parsley, to garnish

1 Heat the oil in a large saucepan. Add the onion, garlic, and leeks and cook gently for 5 minutes, stirring occasionally. Add the flour and cook gently for 1 minute, stirring.

2 Gradually add the broth, stirring, then add all the remaining ingredients except the kidney beans, chick-peas (garbanzo beans), and parsley, and mix well.

3 Bring to the boil, stirring, then cover and simmer for about 30 minutes, until the vegetables are tender, stirring occasionally.

4 Add the beans and chick-peas (garbanzo beans), and stir to mix. Return to the boil and simmer, uncovered, for a further 10 minutes, stirring occasionally.

5 Garnish with chopped parsley and serve on a bed of boiled mixed brown and wild rice.

VARIATIONS
● Use other vegetables of your choice such as mushrooms, parsnips, corn, or succotash.
● Use other canned beans such as black-eyed peas and lima beans in place of the kidney beans and chick-peas (garbanzo beans).
● Use other spices such as curry powder in place of the chili powder.

NUTRITIONAL ANALYSIS
(figures are per serving)

Calories = 256
Fat = 4.3g
of which saturates = 0.5g
          monounsaturates = 1.1g
          polyunsaturates = 1.6g
Protein = 13.8g
Carbohydrate = 43.6g
Dietary fiber = 12.3g
Sodium = 0.6g

Percentage of total calories from fat = 15%
of which saturates = 2%
Percentage of total calories from carbohydrate = 64%
of which sugars = 28%
Good source of fiber & vitamins A, C, & E

LAMB & LENTIL
 # CASSEROLE

This is a filling and nutritious casserole — ideal for warming up those cold winter evenings. Serve it with warmed pita or Armenian bread (lavash) or on a bed of cooked rice or cracked wheat.

Preparation time: 15 minutes

Cooking time: 1 hour

Serves 6

8 ounces lean lamb fillet, cut into small cubes
2 tbsp all-purpose flour, seasoned
1 tsp olive oil
1 onion, sliced
1 clove garlic, crushed
3³/₄ cups beef or vegetable broth
1 cup whole brown or green lentils
1 cup sliced carrots
1¹/₄ cups button mushrooms
8 ounces baby new potatoes, washed
2 sticks celery, chopped
¹/₂ cup peeled, diced rutabaga
¹/₂ cup peeled, diced parsnip
14-ounce can peeled, chopped tomatoes
2 tsp mixed dried herbs
salt and freshly ground black pepper
fresh herb sprigs, to garnish

1 Toss the lamb in the flour. Heat the oil in a large nonstick saucepan and add the lamb, onion, and garlic. Cook for 5 minutes, stirring. Add the remaining flour and cook for 1 minute, stirring.

2 Gradually add the broth, stirring, then add all the remaining ingredients, except the fresh herb sprigs, and mix.

3 Bring to the boil, stirring, then cover and simmer for about 50 minutes, until the lamb, lentils, and vegetables are tender, stirring occasionally.

4 Garnish with fresh herb sprigs and serve with warmed pita or Armenian bread and a chef's salad.

VARIATIONS

● Use other lean meats such as beef, pork, or chicken in place of the lamb.
● Use 1 cup trimmed, sliced leeks in place of the onion.
● Use turnip in place of the rutabaga, and sweet potato or yam, cut in pieces, in place of the new potatoes.

NUTRITIONAL ANALYSIS

(figures are per serving)

Calories = 273
Fat = 5.4g
of which saturates = 1.7g
      monounsaturates = 1.8g
      polyunsaturates = 0.9g

Protein = 20.5g
Carbohydrate = 38.8g
Dietary fiber = 7.4g
Sodium = 0.4g

Percentage of total calories from fat = 18%, of which saturates = 6%
Percentage of total calories from carbohydrate = 53%, of which sugars = 13%
Good source of B vitamins

PORK & LIMA BEAN
BAKE

Serve this layered pork-and-bean bake as a substantial midday or evening meal with some steamed fresh vegetables.

Preparation time: 35 minutes

Cooking time: 1 hour

Serves 6

1 pound potatoes, peeled and thinly sliced
1 tsp sunflower oil
1 1/4 cups lean ground pork
1 large onion, sliced
1 clove garlic, crushed
1 red chili, seeded and finely chopped
2 tbsp all-purpose flour
2 cups chicken or vegetable broth
14-ounce can peeled, chopped tomatoes
1 green bell pepper, seeded and diced
4 celery sticks, chopped
1 cup carrots, thinly sliced
2 leeks, sliced
2 cups canned lima beans, rinsed and drained
14-ounce can pinto beans, rinsed and drained
1 tbsp whole-grain mustard
2 tsp dried sage
2 tsp dried thyme
salt and freshly ground black pepper

1 Parboil the potatoes in a saucepan of lightly salted, boiling water for about 4 minutes. Drain thoroughly and set aside.

2 Heat the oil in a large nonstick saucepan, add the pork, onion, garlic, and chili, and cook for 5 minutes, stirring occasionally. Add the flour and cook for 1 minute, stirring.

3 Gradually add the broth and tomatoes and bring to the boil, stirring. Add all the remaining ingredients and mix together thoroughly.

4 Place half the pork mixture in a lightly greased ovenproof casserole dish and top with an even layer of half the potato slices. Spoon the remaining pork mixture over the potatoes and top with the remaining potato slices to cover the pork completely.

5 Cover with foil and bake in a preheated oven at 400° for 40 minutes. Remove the foil and cook for a further 20 minutes, until the potatoes are lightly browned.

NUTRITIONAL ANALYSIS

(figures are per serving)

Calories = 268
Fat = 4.0g
of which saturates = 0.9g
      monounsaturates = 1.3g
      polyunsaturates = 1.1g
Protein = 20.3g
Carbohydrate = 40.0g
Dietary fiber = 9.1g
Sodium = 0.6g

Percentage of total calories from fat = 14%
of which saturates = 3%
Percentage of total calories from
carbohydrate = 56%, of which sugars = 16%
Good source of B vitamins & vitamins A & C

CHICKEN
MEDLEY

A delicious combination of chicken, fresh vegetables, and beans in a light cheese sauce, topped with crispy potatoes — a family favorite every time.

Preparation time: 35 minutes

Cooking time: 30-45 minutes

Serves 6

2 pounds potatoes, peeled and cut into chunks
2-3 tbsp skim milk
salt and freshly ground black pepper
3 tbsp low-fat spread
3 tbsp all-purpose flour
2 cups low-fat or 2% milk
2 cups chicken broth, cooled
1/2 cup finely grated, reduced-fat Cheddar cheese
1 cup diced cooked, skinless chicken breast
1 onion, minced and blanched
1 clove garlic, crushed
1 1/4 cups mushrooms, sliced
1 cup green beans, halved and blanched
3/4 cup frozen baby lima beans
14-ounce can red kidney beans, rinsed and drained
14-ounce can black-eyed peas, rinsed and drained
3/4 cup canned corn kernels, drained
2-3 tbsp chopped fresh mixed herbs or 2-3 tsp dried mixed herbs
fresh parsley sprigs, to garnish

1 Cook the potatoes in a saucepan of lightly salted, boiling water for 15-20 minutes, until cooked and tender. Drain thoroughly, then mash, and mix with the skim milk and seasoning. Set aside.

2 Meanwhile, place the low-fat spread, flour, milk, and broth in a saucepan and heat gently, whisking continuously, until the sauce comes to the boil and thickens. Simmer gently for

3 minutes, stirring. Remove the pan from the heat.

3 Add the cheese and stir until melted. Add all the remaining ingredients, except the parsley sprigs, adjust the seasoning, and mix well.

4 Spoon the chicken mixture into an ovenproof casserole dish and cover with the creamed potato topping. Make grooves in the top with the tines of a fork.

5 Bake in a preheated oven at 375° for 30-45 minutes, until the potato topping is crisp and browned.

6 Garnish with fresh parsley sprigs and serve with steamed fresh seasonal vegetables such as broccoli flowerets and broiled tomatoes.

VARIATIONS

- Use cooked turkey or lean smoked ham in place of the chicken.
- Use garden peas in place of the fava beans.
- Use chick-peas (garbanzo beans) in place of the black-eyed peas.

NUTRITIONAL ANALYSIS

(figures are per serving)

Calories = 473
Fat = 10.1g
of which saturates = 3.9g
     monounsaturates = 2.0g
     polyunsaturates = 1.9g
Protein = 35.0g
Carbohydrate = 64.6g
Dietary fiber = 9.3g
Sodium = 0.6g

Percentage of total calories from fat = 19%
of which saturates = 8%
Percentage of total calories from carbohydrate = 51%, of which sugars = 10%
Good source of calcium & B vitamins

CHAPTER SEVEN

FRUIT & VEGETABLES

*F*ruit and vegetables are available in many shapes, sizes, colors, and textures.
The range to choose from is vast and most varieties, including exotic items, are
available to be eaten and enjoyed all year round.
Fruit and vegetables are usually served as part of a meal.
They are low in fat and are packed full of a whole range of vitamins and minerals,
such as vitamins A, C, and E, as well as iron and dietary fiber.
Many, such as citrus fruit, salad vegetables, and green vegetables, have a low energy value
and are therefore low in calories and fat. Others, such as dried fruit, root vegetables, peas,
and corn, have a slightly higher energy value, mainly from carbohydrates, which means they
contain slightly more calories, but are still low in fat.
Besides eating them raw, most fruit and vegetables can be cooked in a variety of ways,
including steaming, poaching, baking, broiling, or barbecuing.

CRUNCHY MIXED VEGETABLE
STIR-FRY

*A colorful combination of vegetables quickly stir-fried so that
they remain crunchy, this dish can be served on its own,
or with boiled egg noodles or rice.*

Preparation time: 20 minutes

Cooking time: 15 minutes

Serves 4

1 tsp cornstarch
2 tbsp soy sauce
2 tbsp dry sherry
1 tbsp tomato ketchup
salt and freshly ground black pepper
2 tsp sesame oil
1 clove garlic, crushed
2 leeks trimmed and thinly sliced
1 red bell pepper, seeded and sliced
2 carrots, cut into matchstick strips
2 zucchini, cut into matchstick strips
¹/₂ cup bean sprouts
¹/₂ cup shredded collard greens
¹/₂ cup snow-peas, trimmed

1 Blend the cornstarch with the soy
sauce, sherry, tomato ketchup, and
seasoning. Set aside.

2 Heat the oil in a large nonstick skillet
or wok. Add the garlic, leeks, bell pepper,
carrots, and zucchini and stir-fry over a
high heat for 3-4 minutes.

3 Add the bean sprouts, collard greens,
and snow-peas and stir-fry for 1-2 minutes.

4 Add the cornstarch mixture and stir-fry
for 1-2 minutes. Serve immediately.

VARIATION
● Use a mixture of vegetables of your
choice such as mushrooms, green
peppers, baby corn, onion, cabbage, or
Chinese (Napa) cabbage, and broccoli.

NUTRITIONAL ANALYSIS

(figures are per serving)

Calories = 114
Fat = 2.8g
of which saturates = 0.5g
      monounsaturates = 0.6g
      polyunsaturates = 1.3g
Protein = 5.5g
Carbohydrate = 15.6g
Dietary fiber = 5.6g
Sodium = 0.6g

Percentage of total calories from fat = 22%
of which saturates = 4%
Percentage of total calories from
carbohydrate = 51%
of which sugars = 42%
Good source of vitamins A & C

OVEN-ROASTED ROOT
VEGETABLES

Root vegetables, lightly tossed in flavored oil and oven-roasted until tender and crisp, make an ideal accompaniment to broiled fish or lean meat. Alternatively, they can be served on their own as a lunch or dinnertime snack.

Preparation time: 15 minutes
Cooking time: 1 hour
Serves 4

*1¹/₂ cups sweet potatoes,
peeled and cut into chunks
1¹/₂ cups potatoes, peeled and cut into chunks
1 cup parsnips, peeled and cut into chunks
1 cup rutabaga, peeled and cut into chunks
1 cup celery root, peeled and cut into chunks
3 tbsp olive oil
1 clove garlic, crushed
2 tsp chopped fresh rosemary
salt and freshly ground black pepper
fresh rosemary sprigs, to garnish*

1 Parboil all the vegetables in a large saucepan of lightly salted, boiling water for 3 minutes, then drain thoroughly.

2 In a large bowl, mix together the oil, garlic, rosemary, and seasoning. Toss the vegetables in the oil to coat them lightly all over.

3 Place the vegetables in a roasting pan. Bake in a preheated oven at 425° for 45-60 minutes, until the vegetables are crisp and tender, turning over occasionally.

4 Garnish with fresh rosemary sprigs and serve with broiled fish such as sole or salmon and steamed seasonal fresh vegetables such as garden peas and baby carrots.

VARIATIONS
● Use turnip in place of the rutabaga.
● Use carrots in place of the parsnips.
● Use other herbs such as mixed herbs or thyme in place of the rosemary.
● Use flavored oil such as chili oil or herb oil in place of the olive oil.

NUTRITIONAL ANALYSIS

(figures are per serving)

Calories = 279
Fat = 9.9g
of which saturates = 1.5g
      monounsaturates = 6.3g
      polyunsaturates = 1.2g

Protein = 5.0g
Carbohydrate = 45.0g
Dietary fiber = 6.9g
Sodium = 0.09g

Percentage of total calories from fat = 32%, of which saturates = 5%
Percentage of total calories from carbohydrate = 60%, of which sugars = 21%
Good source of vitamin C

STEAMED CHOCOLATE & CHERRY
PUDDING

A wickedly tempting, light chocolate sponge pudding, topped with a layer of succulent cherries and served with a light chocolate sauce.

Preparation time: 25 minutes
Cooking time: 1¹/₂ hours
Serves 6-8

FOR THE CHOCOLATE PUDDING
14-ounce can pitted cherries in syrup
3 tbsp cocoa powder, sifted
¹/₂ cup soft margarine
¹/₂ cup sugar
2 eggs, beaten
1¹/₂ cups self-rising flour, sifted
¹/₂ cup raisins
skim milk, to mix

FOR THE CHOCOLATE SAUCE
5 tsp cornstarch
1 tbsp cocoa powder
300 ml (¹/₂ pint) low-fat or 2% milk
2 tbsp sugar

1 To make the pudding, drain the cherries, reserving 2 tbsp juice. Place the cherries and the reserved juice in a lightly greased 2¹/₂-pint heatproof bowl. Set aside.

2 In a mixing bowl, blend the cocoa powder with 3 tbsp hot water. Set aside.

3 Cream the fat and sugar together until pale and fluffy. Add the cocoa mixture and mix well. Gradually add the eggs, beating well after each addition.

4 Fold in half the flour, then fold in the remaining flour with the raisins and enough milk to make a soft dropping consistency.

5 Spoon the chocolate mixture over the cherries and level the surface. Cover with a double layer of greased parchment paper or nonstick baking paper, folded to fit securely over the top of the heatproof bowl, and secure with string.

6 Place the bowl in the top half of a steamer over a saucepan of boiling water. Cover with the lid and steam for about 1¹/₂ hours, until the pudding is risen and cooked, topping up the boiling water regularly.

7 Meanwhile, make the chocolate sauce to accompany the pudding. Place the cornstarch and cocoa powder in a saucepan and blend with 3 tbsp milk, to form a smooth paste. Gradually blend in the remaining milk.

8 Heat gently, whisking continuously, until the sauce comes to the boil and thickens. Simmer gently for 2 minutes, stirring. Add the sugar to taste and stir well.

9 Turn the pudding out on a serving plate and serve immediately with the chocolate sauce.

VARIATIONS
● Use yellow raisins or chopped ready-to-eat dried apricots in place of the raisins.
● Use other canned fruits such as peaches or apricots in place of the cherries.
● Serve the pudding with low-fat topping or sauce, or reduced-fat cream, in place of the chocolate sauce.

CARROT & RAISIN
CAKE

*A delicious moist cake, ideal for slicing and packing up
for a mid-morning snack or an afternoon treat.*

Preparation time: 20 minutes
Cooking time: 1-1½ hours
Serves 12

FOR THE CAKE
³/₄ cup low-fat spread
1 cup light soft brown sugar
3 eggs
³/₄ cup all-purpose flour, sifted
³/₄ cup whole-wheat flour, sifted
1 tsp double-acting baking powder
1 tsp baking soda
1 tsp ground mixed spice
1 cup coarsely grated carrots
³/₄ cup yellow raisins
skim milk, to mix

FOR THE FROSTING
1 cup confectioner's (powdered) sugar
1 tsp finely grated lemon rind
1-2 tbsp freshly squeezed lemon juice
pared lemon rind, to decorate

1 Place the low-fat spread, brown sugar, eggs, flours, baking powder, baking soda, and spice in a bowl and beat together until thoroughly mixed.

2 Add the carrots and beat until well mixed. Fold in the yellow raisins and enough milk to make a soft dropping consistency.

3 Turn the mixture into a lightly greased, deep 7-inch round cake pan and level the surface.

4 Bake in a preheated oven at 350° for 1-1½ hours, until firm to the touch and lightly browned.

5 Allow to cool slightly in the pan, then turn out onto a wire rack to cool completely.

6 To make the frosting, sift the sugar into a bowl. Add the lemon rind and gradually add some lemon juice, mixing well — the frosting should be thick enough to coat the back of a spoon.

7 Spread the frosting over the top of the cold cake and decorate with pared lemon rind. Serve in slices.

VARIATIONS
● Use other dried fruits such as chopped, ready-to-eat dried apricots, pears, or peaches in place of the yellow raisins.
● Use white sugar in place of the light soft brown sugar.
● Omit the spice, if preferred.

SPICY FRUIT
COMPOTE

Serve this dish of dried fruit steeped in a fruity sauce flavored with a hint of spice for breakfast, or as a brunch or dessert.

Preparation time: 10 minutes
Serves 4

²/₃ *cup unsweetened orange juice*
²/₃ *cup unsweetened apple juice*
²/₃ *cup dry white wine*
1 tsp ground mixed spice
1¹/₂ cups mixed dried fruits, such as apple rings, peaches, prunes, pears, and apricots
2 tbsp toasted flaked almonds, to decorate

1 In a bowl, mix together the orange juice, apple juice, white wine, and mixed spice.

2 Add the dried fruit and mix well. Cover, chill, and leave to soak in the refrigerator overnight, stirring a couple of times.

3 Serve the fruit compote either chilled or at room temperature, decorated with toasted almonds. Serve on its own or with low-fat ice cream or reduced-fat cream.

VARIATIONS
● The fruit juices, wine, and spice may be heated until boiling and poured over the fruit while hot. The fruit can then be cooled and chilled as above, before serving, or alternatively the compote may be served warm.
● Use a selection of fresh fruits such as peaches, apricots, dates, and oranges, in place of the dried fruits.
● Use other mixtures of fruit juices and wine, such as pineapple juice, grapefruit juice, and rosé wine.

NUTRITIONAL ANALYSIS
(figures are per serving)

Calories = 255
Fat = 4.0g
of which saturates = 0.3g
      monounsaturates = 2.2g
      polyunsaturates = 1.0g

Protein = 3.9g
Carbohydrate = 48.0g
Dietary fiber = 7.1g
Sodium = 0.02g

Percentage of total calories from fat = 14%
of which saturates = 1%
Percentage of total calories from carbohydrate = 71%
of which sugars = 70%
Good source of vitamin C

QUICK IDEAS FOR FRUIT COMPOTES

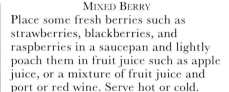

PEACH & PEAR
Mix together some canned or fresh sliced peaches and pears with fruit juices such as apple and orange juice. Add 1 tsp ground mixed spice or nutmeg to taste, and serve warm or cold.

MIXED BERRY
Place some fresh berries such as strawberries, blackberries, and raspberries in a saucepan and lightly poach them in fruit juice such as apple juice, or a mixture of fruit juice and port or red wine. Serve hot or cold.

APRICOT & GRAPE
Slice some fresh or canned apricots and place them in a bowl with some halved red and green seedless grapes. Mix together some pineapple or orange juice, add some light dry or rosé wine (optional), and pour over the fruit. Leave to stand at room temperature or chill for an hour or so before serving.

NUTRITIONAL ANALYSIS
(figures are per serving)

Calories = 234
Fat = 5.3g
of which saturates = 1.5g
       monounsaturates = 2.5g
       polyunsaturates = 0.4g
Protein = 6.2g
Carbohydrate = 42.4g
Dietary fiber = 3.2g
Sodium = 0.04g

Percentage of total calories from fat = 20%
of which saturates = 6%
Percentage of total calories from
carbohydrate = 68%
of which sugars = 60%

BANANA APRICOT FOOL

This dessert made with puréed fruit is quick and easy to make and full of flavor. Serve it on its own, or with some fresh fruit or vanilla wafers.

Preparation time: 15 minutes
Cooking time: 10 minutes
Serves 6

1 cup ready-to-eat dried apricots
2 tbsp sugar
juice of 1 large orange
3 medium bananas
1 package low-fat vanilla dessert, made according to package instructions
²/₃ cup low-fat yogurt
2 tbsp toasted chopped hazelnuts, to decorate

1 Place the apricots, sugar, and orange juice in a saucepan. Cover, bring to the boil, and simmer gently for 10 minutes, stirring occasionally. Remove the pan from the heat and set aside to cool completely.

2 Peel and slice the bananas. Place the bananas and cooled apricot mixture in a blender or food processor and blend until smooth. Add the vanilla dessert and low-fat yogurt and blend until well mixed.

3 Transfer to a serving dish, cover, and chill until ready to serve.

4 Decorate with the hazelnuts and serve with some fresh fruit or wafer biscuits.

VARIATIONS
● Use other dried fruits such as prunes, pears, or peaches in place of the apricots.
● Add 1 tsp ground mixed spice or ginger to the apricots, if liked.
● Use reduced-fat sour cream or sour cream substitute in place of the yogurt.

BANANA BERRY SHAKE

A refreshing and nutritious high-energy shake to enjoy before or after exercise.

Preparation time: 10 minutes
Serves 2

1 banana, peeled and sliced
³/₄ cup strawberries, hulled and halved
1¹/₄ cups low-fat or 2% milk
1 tbsp clear honey

Place the banana and strawberries in a blender or liquidizer and blend until smooth. Add the milk and honey and blend until smooth and well mixed. Pour into glasses and serve immediately.

NUTRITIONAL ANALYSIS

(figures are per serving)

Calories = 169
Fat = 2.7g
of which saturates = 1.6g
    monounsaturates = 0.8g
    polyunsaturates = 0.05g
Protein = 6.2g
Carbohydrate = 31.9g
Dietary fiber = 1.2g
Sodium = 0.09g

Percentage of total calories from fat = 14%
of which saturates = 9%
Percentage of total calories from carbohydrate = 71%, of which sugars = 68%
Good source of vitamin C

PINEAPPLE ORANGE CRUSH

A refreshing thirst quencher, served with crushed ice, that is quick and easy to make.

Preparation time: 10 minutes
Serves 2

8-ounce can pineapple in fruit juice
1¹/₄ cups unsweetened orange juice
crushed ice, to serve
fresh mint sprigs, to decorate

Place the pineapple and juice in a blender or food processor and blend until reasonably smooth. Add the orange juice and blend until well mixed. Add some crushed ice and blend briefly to mix. Pour into glasses and serve immediately. Alternatively, pour the mixture (without the ice) into a pitcher, cover, and refrigerate until required. Stir and serve in glasses with crushed ice.

NUTRITIONAL ANALYSIS

(figures are per serving)

Calories = 108
Fat = 0.2g
of which saturates = 0g
    monounsaturates = 0g
    polyunsaturates = 0g
Protein = 1.1g
Carbohydrate = 27.2g
Dietary fiber = 0.7g
Sodium = 0.02g

Percentage of total calories from fat = 1%
of which saturates = 0%
Percentage of total calories from carbohydrate = 94%, of which sugars = 94%
Good source of vitamin C